"James Goll continues to equip and inspire the Body of Christ in fresh, powerful ways. His newest book is essential reading for believers of all backgrounds—from Gen Z t The Bible declares that you are more th Christ (Romans 8:37). It's time to walk son or daughter of the God who will

Dr. Ché Ahn, senior leader, Harves president, Harvest International Ministry, international chancellor, Wagner University

"James Goll's new book is an excellent compendium on spiritual warfare. For Christians who struggle to grasp the reality of the unseen world, this book describes both the structure of that realm and how we recognize the spiritual assaults that Satan wages against us. James clearly and concisely teaches about our spiritual weapons and how we can fight back unto victory. This is not a book that dwells on the devil's power, but rather on the triumph of the cross."

Ken Fish, founder, Orbis Ministries

"God is displacing the kingdom of darkness today with His own. He is filling the earth with the knowledge of His glory. Heaven's hosts are engaging Satan's, whose time is running short. Friends, we don't fight for victory, but from victory with victory. *The Triumph* will equip you with strategies and empower you to engage in victorious warfare to see the schemes of the enemy pushed back, uprooted, and defeated."

Becca Greenwood, co-founder, Christian Harvest International and Strategic Prayer Apostolic Network

"James Goll has written one of the clearest coverages of the area of spiritual warfare that I know. It is real, biblical, and a joy to read. You will love it and learn how to defeat the devil!"

Cindy Jacobs, co-founder, Generals International

"Jesus lived not in reaction to the devil but in response to the Father. In doing so, He modeled the victorious lifestyle made available to all who follow Him. My friend, James Goll, is one of the most devoted students of the Word I've ever known. Coupling his passion for the Holy Spirit with his devotion to the Word, he penned *The Triumph*, a manual for victory. In this book, he brilliantly conveys the insights needed to walk in the freedom that Jesus obtained for us all. I am certain *The Triumph* will thoroughly equip the reader to live triumphantly."

Bill Johnson, Bethel Church, Redding, CA; author, *Open Heavens* and *The Supernatural Power of a Transformed Mind*

"James Goll is a prophetic pioneer and father in this generation who is blazing a path for the warriors among us. Drawing on decades of overcoming spiritual warfare and gaining strategic prophetic insight, he gives practical wisdom and keys that will bless anyone who reads this new book. I highly recommend it to those who are hungry to triumph over darkness and walk in true kingdom power and authority."

Jeremiah Johnson, founder, the Altar Global,
www.JeremiahJohnson.tv

"*The Triumph* is extremely timely! We are in an era where our invisible enemy, the devil, is working overtime to steal, kill, and destroy. If we are not aware of his tactics and do not become equipped to overcome him, then we will be in a sorry state indeed. We are truly victors in Christ and are called to make a difference as we expel darkness with the weapons of our warfare. Once again, Dr. James Goll has brought a true gift to the Body by sharing the profound and precise revelations of truth contained in this book."

Patricia King, author, minister, media producer, and host

"*The Triumph* answers one of the greatest needs of God's people in this hour, offering an intellectually accessible, biblically and theologically grounded, fresh training in spiritual warfare. *The Triumph* will equip you with practical tools and the hope-filled confidence that Christ has indeed triumphed over every dark power."

Kim Maas, founder/CEO, Kim Maas Ministries; international
speaker; TV and podcast host of *Move Forward
with Dr. Kim Maas*; author of *Prophetic Community,
The Way of the Kingdom*, and *Finding Our Muchness*

"James Goll has penned a masterpiece in *The Triumph*. You were made to war for your portion, on earth as it is in heaven. James takes you from your heavenly abiding place and helps you learn to stand in your earthly domain with the Anointed One who defeated and destroyed your foes. You will be dressed to fight. *The Triumph* is an instruction manual that will teach you to clothe yourself properly for the war now and in the days ahead. This book is a must to prepare you to win in the journey called LIFE!"

Dr. Chuck D. Pierce, president, Glory of Zion International,
Kingdom Harvest Alliance

THE
TRIUMPH

Other Chosen Books by James W. Goll

Deliverance from Darkness
The Mystery of Israel and the Middle East
Hearing God's Voice Today
Praying with God's Heart
The Lifestyle of a Prophet
The Lifestyle of a Watchman
Living a Supernatural Life

THE
TRIUMPH

YOUR COMPREHENSIVE GUIDE TO
SPIRITUAL WARFARE

JAMES W. GOLL

Chosen
a division of Baker Publishing Group
Minneapolis, Minnesota

© 2024 by James W. Goll

Published by Chosen Books
Minneapolis, Minnesota
ChosenBooks.com

Chosen Books is a division of
Baker Publishing Group, Grand Rapids, Michigan

Printed in the United States of America

ISBN 9780800763220 (paper)
ISBN 9780800772758 (casebound)
ISBN 9781493441044 (ebook)

Library of Congress Cataloging-in-Publication Control Number: 2023046712

Unless otherwise indicated, Scripture quotations are taken from the (NASB®) New American Standard Bible®, Copyright © 1960, 1971, 1977, 1995, 2020 by The Lockman Foundation. Used by permission. All rights reserved. www.lockman.org

Scripture quotations identified AMP are taken from the Amplified Bible, Copyright © 1954, 1958, 1962, 1964, 1965, 1987 by The Lockman Foundation. Used by permission.

Scripture quotations identified KJV are from the King James Version of the Bible.

Scripture quotations identified MSG are taken from *The Message*, copyright © 1993, 2002, 2018 by Eugene H. Peterson. Used by permission of NavPress. All rights reserved. Represented by Tyndale House Publishers.

Scripture quotations identified NIV are taken from the Holy Bible, New International Version®, NIV®. Copyright © 1973, 1978, 1984, 2011 by Biblica, Inc.® Used by permission of Zondervan. All rights reserved worldwide. www.zondervan.com. The "NIV" and "New International Version" are trademarks registered in the United States Patent and Trademark Office by Biblica, Inc.®

Scripture quotations identified NKJV are taken from the New King James Version®. Copyright © 1982 by Thomas Nelson. Used by permission. All rights reserved.

Scripture quotations identified NLT are taken from the *Holy Bible*, New Living Translation, copyright © 1996, 2004, 2015 by Tyndale House Foundation. Used by permission of Tyndale House Publishers, Carol Stream, Illinois 60188. All rights reserved.

Scripture quotations identified TLB are taken from *The Living Bible*, copyright © 1971 by Tyndale House Foundation. Used by permission of Tyndale House Foundation, Carol Stream, Illinois 60188. All rights reserved.

Scripture quotations identified TPT are from The Passion Translation®. Copyright © 2017, 2018, 2020 by Passion & Fire Ministries, Inc. Used by permission. All rights reserved. ThePassionTranslation.com.

Cover design by Rob Williams, InsideOut Creative Arts, Inc.

Baker Publishing Group publications use paper produced from sustainable forestry practices and postconsumer waste whenever possible.

24 25 26 27 28 29 30   7 6 5 4 3 2 1

DEDICATION

Over the years I have had the honor of participating in various movements of the Holy Spirit and thus gleaning from strategic international leaders, each one carrying distinct biblical and revelatory understandings. With this in mind, I wish to dedicate *The Triumph: Your Comprehensive Guide to Spiritual Warfare* to three fathers in the faith whose imprint is upon these pages.

First and foremost, to Derek Prince,
the teacher of teachers of the charismatic
movement, who pioneered the way.

Secondly, to C. Peter Wagner,
who brought forth distinct applications and
models for the global prayer movement.

Lastly, to Ed Silvoso,
who defined language and integrated approaches
to empower the Ekklesia to move forward.

May this book be a tool that will help people grow
so they can be enforcers of the victory of Calvary!

CONTENTS

FOREWORD

James Goll's *The Triumph* is one of the most captivating and illuminating books I've read on the topic of spiritual warfare, and because of how it shows us to overcome, I believe it is destined to be a major landmark in Christendom.

James is a personal friend who I trust and admire, a true general in the Kingdom who has experienced spiritual warfare firsthand, facing battles on many fronts, often under perplexing circumstances; he has never given in or given up. He understands and epitomizes the truth that war is not the *end* but the *means* to a life of victory through Christ Jesus our Lord.

The approach James has taken in this book is brilliant and will appeal to believers of all ages and levels of understanding. I'm eager to get copies into the hands of the Millennial, Gen Z, and Gen Alpha generations, since they will need to be equipped for the spiritual battle in culture today more than ever before. The biblical truths contained in the book's three sections—"The Great Battle," "Our Spiritual Weapons," and "Enforcing Christ's Victory"—are presented in contemporary, practical language and organized in a way that helps readers easily apply what they're learning. I encourage you to pay close attention to the "For Reflection and Prayer" section at the end of each chapter.

We are exhorted in Ephesians 6:13 (NKJV) to "take up the whole armor of God, that [we] may be able to withstand in the evil day." Praise be to God that He has equipped us with weapons that are powerful and effective, and that if we stand firm and do not give up, we will see the Day of the Lord, a triumphant victory that brings glory and honor to our God. This book brilliantly points the way.

Dr. Ed Silvoso
Founder, Transform Our World
Author, *Ekklesia* and *Anointed for Business*

Acknowledgments

Every book is always a team effort. The older I get, the more aware I am of this reality. I am a very limited man. God gives grace to the weak, and some of that grace is manifested in and through other people God has put around me. This book has taken years to compose. It started out as a detailed class called "War in the Heavenlies," which I taught after we first moved from Kansas City to Nashville. Yes, that became one of many study guides with a red cover and black ink accompanied by about twenty scratchy audio cassette tape messages.

So where do I begin to give acknowledgements? Let's start with the many different board and staff members of Ministry to the Nations, which emerged into God Encounters Ministries. I want to give a special thank you to Jeffrey Thompson, who has served this ministry for twenty years. He has served every area of this ministry with excellence. Thank you for holding up my hands. Several years later, I began to teach online classes in partnership with Empower 2000 and their many different team members. Thank you for your partnership!

Then there was the task of turning my outlines and transcripts into a working manuscript. Gratitude goes to Angela Shears, who took all these concepts and helped me shape them into the original manuscript.

Then through a dream I was given the idea of reformatting the entire book into a new style of writing that I had never done before, and also to rebrand it! Thankfully, the team at Baker Publishing Group agreed and assigned their colleague, and my friend of years, David Sluka, to be the editor for this complex task. I cannot begin to express how deeply grateful I am to this man of God for his heart of devotion to the Lord Jesus Christ and for his many hours of perseverance and faithfulness.

Thank you to each and every one.

Introduction

YOU WERE BORN FOR BATTLE

You were born into a war—no matter where or when you were born—and you were born to claim victory in that war. You don't even have to volunteer to participate in this ongoing battle. Just by being born you are caught right in the middle of it!

This fact doesn't sound like great news at first, but the more you learn about the war, the better the news gets. You have been given the privilege of choosing which side to fight for; and when you choose to follow Jesus, you are automatically on the winning side!

How can I be so sure of that outcome? Because of Jesus' marvelous victory at Calvary. When our lovely Messiah hung on the cross, cursed for the sins of the world, He uttered the words, "It is finished!" These are three of the greatest words ever expressed, which have echoed gloriously throughout history. "It is finished!" The work of the cross of Christ was, is, and will continue to be perfectly complete!

And now, as followers of Jesus, we are called to enforce the triumph of Christ upon the powers of darkness. Not only have we been set free from the penalty of sin, sickness, and eternal death, but we also get to be used by the Holy Spirit as a part of God's end-time army to set other captives free. Now *that* is great news!

But to be real with you, there is some boot-camp training necessary if you are going to be a victorious warrior in God's army. Why? Because when you go into battle with the enemy, he strikes back. As you probably know from your spiritual journey thus far, it is helpful to have a guide to assist you as you head into unfamiliar and dangerous territory.

This book is full of excellent teachings extracted from our ultimate guide—God's Word, the Bible—and is divided into three sections: The Great Battle, Our Spiritual Weapons, and Enforcing Christ's Victory. I have purposefully divided each section into smaller chapters so that each chapter can focus on one primary topic, encouraging you to take away one key learning and then apply it to your life. It is those who hear the Word and put it into practice that are able to withstand the great rains, floods, and winds that beat against our houses (see Matthew 7:24–27).

While I'm excited to present to you this comprehensive guide to spiritual warfare, I'm even more excited for you to use these tools to enforce Christ's victory in your everyday life. My prayer is that you will be so heavily armed with the Word of God that when the enemy marches toward you, you can stand firm and strong, resisting every evil attack. May the warrior's mantle come upon you, and may you be filled with this revelation: Greater is He who is in and with you, than he who is in the world (see 1 John 4:4).

May grace be poured out upon you as you march into training camp and then demonstrate the victory of Christ for the glory of our Captain, Commander, and King—Christ Jesus the Lord!

Blessings to you!
James W. Goll

PART 1

The Great Battle

WARRING KINGDOMS

For our struggle is not against flesh and blood, but against the rulers, against the powers, against the world forces of this darkness, against the spiritual forces of wickedness in the heavenly places.

Ephesians 6:12

Let's get real. Some of us have been knocked around pretty hard during our journeys in following Jesus. I sure have! But ultimately, we are all overcomers in Him. In this first section we will look at the great battle every person on earth is born into.

Unfortunately, many of us have been taught and sometimes act like there is no spiritual struggle at all. We take the first part of Ephesians 6:12 (KJV) and stop after "For we wrestle not." We are ignorant of Satan's schemes and believe there is no battle at all, or we enter the battle passively because we believe that Jesus has already triumphed—and if Jesus has done it all, then why do we need to do anything more?

Yes, we enter into the completed work that Jesus has already accomplished. But look at what Paul the apostle actually wrote: "For we do not wrestle against flesh and blood" (NKJV). So guess what? Your spouse is not your enemy. Your boss is not your enemy. And the leader of your country is not your enemy either.

The enemy is the devil (also called Satan, Lucifer, and other names that we'll explore in chapter 3), his demonic forces, and other manipulative spirits of darkness. We do not wrestle with or against flesh and blood in spiritual warfare.

1

THE GREAT BATTLE BETWEEN TWO KINGDOMS

As there is the Kingdom of God, there is also the kingdom of Satan. Let me state clearly from the beginning that Satan is not a king. Satan is a prince who masquerades as a king with a domain or "kingdom" that opposes the one and only true King. These two kingdoms—one true Kingdom and one false kingdom—are in direct conflict with one another.

I personally witnessed this ongoing stark conflict when I led a ministry team from the United States to the island nation of Haiti in the Caribbean. This now poverty-stricken land was once so prosperous and a gem of natural beauty that it was called the Pearl of the Antilles. But through a pact overtly made with the devil, it had become one of the most enslaved and oppressed countries in the world and the poorest country in the Western hemisphere.

Evangelist Mahesh Chavda, a dear friend, was preaching the evening meetings with signs and wonders following as I led our team in round-the-clock prayer and fasting. Our meetings were gaining momentum, both attendance and in shifting the spiritual atmosphere over the dark land. As a result, we heard that a voodoo priest announced over the country's national radio, "All the witch doctors across the nation must gather together at our known place and time because our kingdom is under siege!" Truly this announcement was a direct result of the Kingdom of God making a significant impact on the spiritual battlefield in Haiti.

We were in the middle of a clash in the battle of warring kingdoms! Despite great spiritual resistance, many came to faith. The blind saw, the deaf heard, and Jesus was magnified!

Jesus walked upon our spiritual battlefield while He lived on earth. For example, on a Sabbath He and His disciples walked through some grainfields, and because His disciples were hungry, they broke off some heads of grain and ate them. The Pharisees chastised them and spouted religious rules at Him. Jesus' response?

"Have you not read what David did when he became hungry, he and his companions—how he entered the house of God, and they ate the consecrated bread, which was not lawful for him to eat nor for those with him, but for the priests alone? Or have you not read in the Law that on the Sabbath the priests in the temple violate the Sabbath, and yet are innocent? But I say to you that something greater than the temple is here. But if you had known what this means: 'I DESIRE COMPASSION, RATHER THAN SACRIFICE,' you would not have condemned the innocent."

Matthew 12:3–7

Jesus was well aware of the opposing force while He walked the earth. We must also be aware.

Later that same day, the Pharisees asked Jesus if it was lawful to heal on the Sabbath, hoping to charge Him with a crime. Jesus declared that "the Son of Man is Lord of the Sabbath" (Matthew 12:8), and He proceeded to heal a man with a withered hand as well as a demon-possessed man who was blind and unable to speak— all of which angered the Pharisees so much that they conspired to destroy Him (see Matthew 12:9–24; John 10:10). Knowing their thoughts, Jesus said to them,

> "Every kingdom divided against itself is laid waste; and no city or house divided against itself will stand. And if Satan is casting out Satan, he has become divided against himself; how then will his kingdom stand? And if by Beelzebul I cast out the demons, by whom do your sons cast them out? Therefore, they will be your judges. But if I cast out the demons by the Spirit of God, then the kingdom of God has come upon you."
>
> Matthew 12:25–28

Few Christians fully realize the extent of Satan's influence. Nor do they understand, or exercise, Christ's authority over the enemy. We profess being children of God as the first part of 1 John 5:19 (NIV) tells us: "We know that we are children of God." But rarely do we acknowledge the last part of that important verse: "the whole world is under the control [power] of the evil one." The Greek word used here for "world" is *cosmos*, which means the world system or worldly order of things. (This is not to be confused with the "earth" used in Psalm 24:1, "The earth is the LORD's, and all it contains.") God sends us forth as empowered believers with His Holy Spirit to go into this world system and shine the light of the Good News of Jesus Christ. Remember, light always overcomes darkness!

Of the two warring kingdoms, we can take refuge in and comfort from 1 John 4:4 (NKJV): "You are of God, little children, and have overcome them; because He who is in you is greater than he who is in the world."

Two Ditches to Avoid

There is no neutral ground in spiritual warfare. There are only two opposing armies on the battlefield: dedicated disciples of the Lord Jesus Christ and the heavenly hosts of warring angels versus the army of Satan with its legions of demonic partners. As you take your stand on God's side, I caution you to be aware of the two ditches we can fall into along our way if we are not careful: preoccupation and complacent indifference.

When we are preoccupied with anything other than living for God while fighting against Satan, the enemy can slip through and infiltrate our "mind-field." Likewise, if we are complacent or oblivious to how sly and conniving the enemy is, it won't be long before we're raising the white flag of surrender. God forbid. C. S. Lewis said:

> There are two equal and opposite errors into which our race can fall about the devils. One is to disbelieve in their existence. The other is to believe, and to feel an excessive and unhealthy interest in them. They themselves [i.e., the demons] are equally pleased by both errors, and hail a materialist or a magician with the same delight.[1]

In the physical world, warring kingdoms can be between neighbors, businesses, political parties, countries, even churches. In the spiritual realm, only two warring kingdoms exist—good and evil (see Genesis 2:9, 17). This war has raged since the first Adam, and it continues today. The Last Adam, Jesus, has secured and proclaimed victory for us with His sacrifice on the cross. Hallelujah!

Ephesians 6:12 (paraphrased) says, "Our struggle is not against people; we are wrestling against rulers, powers, forces of darkness, spiritual rulers and spirits of wickedness in heavenly places." Considering all that, let's look at five statements we must understand if we are going to stand strong, persevere, and end up on the side of the triumph of Christ.

Five Strategic Foundational Statements

The following five certainties about spiritual warfare carry through this entire book. I urge you to keep these truths in mind while you read, as they are the basis for understanding the continuing conflict you face and how you can walk in victory in your Christian life.

1. We are born *in* war and born *for* war.
2. All true spiritual warfare centers on God's Son, Jesus Christ.
3. You were created to bring pleasure to God.
4. The source of all spiritual warfare is the root of rebellion.
5. One of the most powerful weapons of spiritual warfare is forgiveness.

Now let's examine each statement briefly.

1. We are born in war and born for war. You didn't ask to be born. No one did. Yet as a child of God, you yourself are a weapon—a mighty weapon in the Lord's hands of spiritual warfare. You are, therefore, up for the task. You are born to fight spiritual battles in the war against evil and be an overcomer for God's glory.

2. All true spiritual warfare centers on God's Son, Jesus Christ. If you look at the fall of Lucifer and his "I will" statements as recorded in Isaiah 14:13–14, his focus is on God and his desire to exalt himself above Him. All true spiritual warfare does not center on you; it centers on the placement of the Son of God in your life, in your family, in your city, and in the nations. That is a strategic foundational truth.

3. You were created to bring pleasure to God. Do you believe that you were created to bring pleasure to God? You may be wondering why I am making such a statement when the topic is spiritual warfare. I say this because it is true and believing it will help you in spiritual warfare. Many believers become weary as heavy-laden prayer warriors with significant burdens in life weighing heavy on their spirit. Yet the Bible says life is not supposed to be a drudgery. Deuteronomy 23:5 says, "The LORD your God turned the curse into a blessing for you because the LORD your God loves you." Numbers 14:8 tells us, "The LORD delights in us, then He will bring us into this land and give it to us, 'a land which flows with milk and honey.'" And Isaiah 66:14 says, "Then you will see this, and your heart will be glad, and your bones will flourish like the new grass." I exhort you to transfer that gladness over to life, realizing that God looks upon you with pleasure, period.

4. The source of all spiritual warfare is the root of rebellion. Disobedience is doing our own will and not the will of God. It is a form of rebellion and the cause of all unrest and conflict. Unfortunately, the world is full of rebellious deeds performed by rebellious societies, cultures, systems, and individuals. We will look at this statement in chapter 3.

5. One of the most powerful weapons of spiritual warfare is forgiveness. Forgiveness is walking in the opposite spirit of evil. Forgiveness is walking in the principles of Jesus' Sermon on the Mount (see Matthew 5–7). One of the most powerful weapons of spiritual warfare that disarms the powers of darkness is forgiveness. Forgiveness really is the foundational basis of our triumph in spiritual warfare.

Remember, wars are finite, but God's Kingdom is eternal. Warring is not the end but the means to live victoriously in Christ.

——— FOR REFLECTION AND PRAYER ———

- Where do you have the most room to grow in your attention to spiritual warfare—engage more because you have been mostly indifferent, or focus on it differently because you have been overly preoccupied?
- When you face hard times or opposition, do you find yourself attributing resistance most often to people (flesh and blood) or a spiritual enemy?
- Which of the five foundational statements of spiritual warfare do you most confidently believe?

Take a few moments right now to talk to God about which of the five foundational statements of spiritual warfare you feel He wants to strengthen in your life at this time.

2

THE NATURE OF CONFLICT AND WARFARE

I used to spend a lot of time in the five boroughs of NYC, investing hundreds of hours in prayer walks, talking to God about the condition of one of America's gateway cities. So it's easy for me to picture a taxi driving out of the maze of the Big Apple of Manhattan, New York City, at 5:00 p.m. Which are you most likely to see when you look out the window? Serene parks with water fountains, block after block, with couples holding hands, strolling on walking paths lined with beautiful flowers? Or thousands of cars jamming the streets with people darting through traffic at the crosswalks trying not to get run over?

When you drive through New York City at rush hour, you must be properly prepared, and you should expect hectic traffic or you will end up in a frenzy! In the same way, you need to be realistically prepared in your daily life and should expect spiritual conflict in life—not just a walk in the park—because that is the nature of the world we live in. According to the Bible, conflict and warfare are normal aspects of our lives. So you'd better be on the alert and you'd better be prepared!

Let's look at an assortment of Scripture passages that show the nature of our battle.

- Second Corinthians 10:3–5 (NIV) says that although "we live in the world, we do not wage war as the world does. The weapons we fight with are not the weapons of the world." This passage addresses the battlefield of our mind, our thoughts, and that our spiritual weapons "have divine power to demolish strongholds. We demolish arguments and every pretension that sets itself up against the knowledge of God, and we take captive every thought to make it obedient to Christ." **Spiritual enemies require spiritual weapons and divine power. God gives us spiritual weapons to fight our battles.**

- First Timothy 1:18 (NKJV) says that when you recall Scripture prophecies, "you may wage the good warfare." **Absorbing God's Word before each battle is vital for a victorious outcome.**

- Second Timothy 2:3–4 (NKJV) declares we must "endure hardship as a good soldier of Jesus Christ. No one engaged in warfare entangles himself with the affairs of this life, that he may please him who enlisted him as a soldier." **With Christ as our Commander in Chief, we have His authority to waylay every enemy.**

- Ephesians 6:12 (NIV) tells us that we struggle "against the rulers, against the authorities, against the powers of this dark world and against the spiritual forces of evil in the heavenly realms." **We must always remember who the real enemy is.**

Have you wondered if you were the only one going through this fight? The only one battling for good when evil seems to surround you? Dear friend, the struggle is a normal part of the Christian life. You're not abnormal. You're not even elite. What you are experiencing is part of what believers contend with.

God as a Victorious Leader

An often-overlooked dimension of God's nature is that He is a victorious leader in every spiritual battle. God is presented to us as a military commander, signifying warring factions, soldiers, weaponry, and all that war entails. In Exodus 15:1–3 (NKJV), the children of Israel sang to the Lord that He had "triumphed gloriously!" and that "The LORD is a man of war." In Joshua 5:13–14 (NKJV), God is called the "Commander of the army of the LORD."

According to Isaiah 13:4 (NKJV), "the LORD of hosts musters the army for battle." "The LORD of hosts" is a reference to an entire company of angels. "The LORD of hosts" is the terminology of King James and New King James versions of the Bible and I prefer this terminology. Some of the more modern translations use "LORD Almighty" and "LORD of Heaven's Armies."

God's presence, power, and character are all contained within His names. The Bible is full of a great variety of God's names. Let's look at them, and then look forward to a more in-depth examination in a later chapter.

There are 140 names cited in God's Word for the Son of God. I have chosen 50 of these marvelous names that each highlight a particular aspect of the nature of God in spiritual warfare. I encourage you to read the Scripture associated with each name and study each one. Let the Holy Spirit reveal to you who Jesus is. Each name reveals an aspect of Jesus' nature. For the ultimate learning experience, pray these scriptures from your heart.

1. Seed of the woman (Genesis 3:15)
2. Rock of Salvation (Deuteronomy 32:15)
3. God's Anointed (Psalm 2:2)
4. Sanctuary (Isaiah 8:14)

5. Counselor (Isaiah 9:6 NKJV)

6. Mighty God (Isaiah 9:6 NKJV)

7. Everlasting Father (Isaiah 9:6 NKJV)

8. Prince of Peace (Isaiah 9:6 NKJV)

9. Chosen One (Isaiah 42:1)

10. Redeemer (Isaiah 59:20)

11. Angel of His Presence (Isaiah 63:9)

12. Lord Our Righteousness (Jeremiah 23:6)

13. Messiah, the Prince (Daniel 9:25; John 4:25)

14. Sun of Righteousness (Malachi 4:2)

15. Christ/Messiah (Matthew 1:17; 2:4 KJV)

16. Emmanuel (God with us) (Matthew 1:23 KJV)

17. King of the Jews (Matthew 2:2; 21:5)

18. Son of the Most High (Luke 1:32)

19. Salvation (Luke 2:30)

20. The Word (John 1:1–2)

21. True Light (John 1:9)

22. Savior of the World (John 4:42)

23. Light of the World (John 8:12)

24. The Way, the Truth, the Life (John 14:6)

25. Lord of All (Acts 10:36)

26. The Deliverer (Romans 11:26)

27. The Power of God (1 Corinthians 1:24)

28. Lord of Glory (1 Corinthians 2:8)

29. Our Passover (1 Corinthians 5:7)

30. Mediator (1 Timothy 2:4–5)

31. Ransom for All (1 Timothy 2:6)

32. Blessed Hope (Titus 2:13)

33. Great God and Savior (Titus 2:13)

34. Radiance of His Glory (Hebrews 1:3)

35. Upholder of All Things (Hebrews 1:3 KJV)

36. Captain of Salvation (Hebrews 2:10 NKJV)
37. Testator (Mediator) of a New Covenant (Hebrews 9:16–17 NKJV)
38. Author and Finisher of Faith (Hebrews 12:2)
39. Great Shepherd of the Sheep (Hebrews 13:20)
40. Shepherd and Guardian of Souls (1 Peter 2:25)
41. Jesus Christ the Righteous (1 John 2:1)
42. Faithful Witness (Revelation 1:5)
43. Ruler of the Kings of the Earth (Revelation 1:5)
44. Alpha and Omega (Revelation 1:8; 21:6; 22:13)
45. The Beginning and the End (Revelation 1:8 NKJV)
46. Origin of Creation (Revelation 3:14; Ephesians 3:9; Colossians 1:15–18)
47. Lion of the Tribe of Judah (Revelation 5:5)
48. The Word of God (Revelation 19:13)
49. King of all kings, Lord of all lords (Revelation 19:16 NLT)
50. Bright and Morning Star (Revelation 22:16 KJV)

This list of God's names highlights aspects of His divine attributes that reveal He is our victorious Champion who always leads us into triumph. Yes, He is a compassionate Warrior for each one of us in all the circumstances we face in our lives. We also know from God's Word that there is most definitely a battle raging in the heavenlies—and that He is the triumphant Leader and glorious Victor of the prevailing forces. Amen and amen!

FOR REFLECTION AND PRAYER

- To what degree are you aware of the spiritual battle you are in each day? Do you expect it, or are you surprised or disappointed by it?

- When you consider the nature of God, what attributes usually first come to your mind?
- How does God's nature as a victorious, warring leader affect how you see Him?

Take a few moments right now to relook at the names of Jesus listed above. Identify three to five that are especially meaningful to you currently and call out to God using those names.

3

THE ARCHENEMY OF GOD

Satan, the devil, is clearly described as the enemy of God through-out the entire Bible. Pride was found in the heart of this created one as he compared himself with himself. Lucifer aspired to be equal with, or even transcend to be above, the Creator Himself.

As he attempted to rise above the other leading archangels, who apparently were content to remain in their majestic roles, he slipped. He lost his function and role in what the Bible calls the third heaven, which is where God dwells. The cosmic war of the ages was on. God, the Creator, now had an enemy. One of His own had now broken ranks and decided to wage war against the Lord and His anointed!

This enemy has many names in God's Book, including the fol-lowing fourteen:

1. The word *Satan* is cited fifty-four times in the New King James Bible. The word literally means "the adversary," the one who opposes. In Job 1:6–9, 12; 2:1–4, 6, 7, "the one who opposes" is not so much a name as it is a description of Satan's character and activity. More than any other

phrase or word, the name *Satan* is used to describe the enemy of God.

2. *Devil* or *diabolos* is cited thirty-four times in the New Testament of the New King James Bible and literally means "slanderer, accuser." Note especially Luke 4:2, 13 and Revelation 12:9, 12 where it is the devil's aim to defame. He is a constant source of false and malicious reports.

3. *Lucifer* literally means "shining one." I'm going to push pause on this name because in the following chapters, we discuss the creation, the fall, and the rebellion of Lucifer, particularly described in Isaiah 14.

4. *Old serpent* is cited in Revelation 12:9, 15, an obvious allusion to Genesis 3. Compare 2 Corinthians 11:3 and Romans 16:20, which says, "The God of peace will soon crush Satan [old serpent] under your feet."

5. *Great dragon* is cited in Revelation 12:3, 7, 9, 17 and presented as a terrifying, destructive beast.

6. *Ruler* or *prince of this world* is mentioned in John 12:31; 14:30; 16:11. I explore this term in detail in my book *Strike the Mark*.

7. *Ruler* or *prince of the power of the air* is cited in Ephesians 2:2. Satan rules over a spiritual domain that centers on and operates in the earth's atmosphere.

8. *God of this age*: 2 Corinthians 4:4 (see also Psalm 24:1; 89:11).

9. *Evil one* or *wicked one*: Matthew 6:13; 13:38; John 17:15; 1 John 2:14; 5:18.

10. *Prince/ruler of demons*; *Beelzebub/Belial*: Matthew 10:25; 12:26; Luke 11:15; 2 Corinthians 6:15. The name/title *Beelzebub* means "lord of the flies," a title given to one of the pagan gods of the Philistines, brought over into Judaism as a name for Satan. More graphically it means "god of filth."

11. *Destroyer*: Revelation 9:11. Also known as *Abaddon* in Hebrew meaning "ruin, destruction," or *Apollyon* in Greek meaning "exterminator, destroyer."
12. *Tempter*: Matthew 4:3; 1 Thessalonians 3:5.
13. *Accuser*: Revelation 12:10.
14. *Deceiver*: Revelation 12:9; 20:3.

These names are synonymous with evil and are the very essence of what Satan's dark realm stands for. He is the mortal enemy of God's children. There is nothing good or redeemable in the oppressor, no room for compromise or capitulation.

Standing strong on the opposite side of the demarcation line must be believers in Jesus, knowing that God's Kingdom stands for love, light, justice, righteousness, peace, joy, and everything good (see Romans 14:17, Hebrews 1:8, and others).

In addition to the enemy's names and attributes I've listed, the results of Lucifer's rebellion and fall are also evident when examining his nature and various characteristics.

- Satan is a master of misrepresentation. Consider him the leader of the masquerade party. Yes, it's the truth (see 2 Thessalonians 2:9 and 2 Corinthians 11:14–15).
- The devil is powerful but not omnipotent (see Matthew 4:5, 8). Only God is all-powerful. Satan, a fallen angel, is not all-powerful.
- Satan is intelligent but not omniscient. Only God has all knowledge. The enemy has a realm of knowledge, and he tries to grow in knowledge, but only God has all knowledge.
- The devil is active but not omnipresent. Only God is omnipresent; He is everywhere at all times. Satan does not have the capacity to be everywhere at all times.

Rebellion Is the Cause of All Unrest and Conflict

The simple truth is that rebellion is the cause of all unrest and conflict. The refusal to submit to the righteous government of God is the source of warring. Unfortunately, the world is full of rebellious deeds performed by rebellious societies, cultures, systems, and individual people.

Countries worldwide have been living and dying in the midst of earthly physical wars as well as heavenly spiritual wars for many centuries. A great paradox exists that should not be. Seoul, South Korea, has been known for years as hosting one of the world's largest churches, with over 800,000 believers. That great move of the Holy Spirit had its beginning over a hundred years before in the northern part of Korea in Pyongyang, which is now under a fierce, atheistic, communist dictatorship. Somehow that root of rebellion against God and His ways continues to raise its head! The battle of light and darkness continues.

Nigeria is known for its great number of believers. There are many megachurches, and the world's largest prayer gatherings of over one million people take place in this beloved nation. Yet, Nigeria is also known for some of the greatest governmental corruption, crime, and deception in the world. How can this be? Light and darkness coexist in this country, and the same scenario is played out in other countries as well.

To bring God's Kingdom to earth, we must be willing to lead the way, calling forth practical applications that generate not only sporadic revivals, but also a revival culture that manifests transformed lives that will revolutionize communities, governmental systems, education, and nations. We must do more than preach the Gospel of salvation; we must model the Gospel of transformation!

You Have Been Empowered to Walk in Victory

In Matthew 6:9–10 (KJV), we are taught how to pray by our Lord Jesus Christ: "Thy kingdom come, Thy will be done in earth, as it is in heaven." How does His Kingdom and His will begin to manifest on earth? It begins with you and me rejecting rebellion and rebellious acts of disobedience.

Habakkuk 2:13–14 (NLT) says: "Has not the LORD of Heaven's Armies promised that the wealth of nations will turn to ashes? They work so hard, but all in vain! For as the waters fill the sea, the earth will be filled with an awareness of the glory of the LORD." While teaching on this verse years ago, I heard the Holy Spirit ask me, "How is the glory of the Lord going to cover the earth as the waters cover the seas?" I have learned during my journey that when God asks a question, it's not because He doesn't have the answer. Every question is an invitation into participation.

I now know to turn the question back to God, so while yet teaching, I responded, "Okay, God, how?" And a very simple answer came to me, "One clay pot at a time." So, "Thy Kingdom come, Thy will be done" begins with me. It begins with you.

I have a question for you. What action steps will you take to bring implementation to the triumph of Christ's spiritual warfare? Will you remain waiting on God to do something spectacular, or could it be that He is waiting for you to do something simple and practical with what He has already accomplished?

FOR REFLECTION AND PRAYER

- What aspect of the nature of the enemy has confronted you the most in your life? In other words, what do most of his attacks look like?
- Where have you found success against the enemy, and where have you felt defeated?
- How have you struggled with rebellion?

◆ ◆ ◆ ◆

At the close of each of the twelve spiritual warfare topics, I will also include a victorious spiritual warfare prayer. I encourage you to pray it out loud, with courage and strength. Remember, the Kingdom of God is a speech-activated Kingdom. So, say it once, pray it twice, and declare it a third time!

VICTORIOUS SPIRITUAL WARFARE PRAYER

Father God, in the mighty name of Jesus, I come before You, knowing You have empowered me for victory. From the very beginning of time, I was born into the midst of a great cosmic war. I was born to participate in spiritual warfare, which is required to advance Your will and Kingdom on earth.

The devil is a liar, a usurper, and a thief, and all he has ever done is steal, kill, and destroy. But You, Jesus, are the Man of War, revealing Yourself in Your Word as the King and the Captain of the Lord's army, ruling over principalities and powers of darkness.

You, Lord, are my Commander, and I will follow Your lead and obey Your commandments. Make me a vessel of Your glory. I declare that greater are You who is with me, than those who are with the enemy. You, God, are victorious, and I am grateful to be on the winning side with You. Amen and amen!

LUCIFER'S REBELLION

How you are fallen from heaven, O shining star, son of the morning! You have been thrown down to the earth, you who destroyed the nations of the world.

Isaiah 14:12 NLT

We—humans on earth—are not alone. Angels, demons, and other supernatural beings are also present and interact with our world. To understand spiritual warfare properly, you need to understand the realm of the angelic hosts.

I have studied the three hundred verses in the Bible concerning angels for over three decades. I have also read or gleaned from more than one hundred books by credible authors when I did my study for this book on spiritual warfare and research for the book *Angelic Encounters Today*.

My intense research opened the door for my home to become a place of angelic habitation. For nine weeks in a row, my late wife, Michal Ann, and I experienced angelic visitations that started at midnight and concluded at five o'clock in the morning. These visitations centered around Michal Ann, and each encounter was mind-blowing.

The sixty-four early-morning visitations included fiery seraphim, a deliverance by the fiery host, messenger angels bringing us revelation, hearing choirs of angels singing, and much more. I know these realms. My late wife, Michal Ann, walked in these realms. I feel compelled to share with you some of what I learned so you can grow in your knowledge about these celestial beings and engage in spiritual warfare more effectively God's way.

4

ANGELS 101

Can angels be seen, felt, and experienced today like they were in Bible times? Well, guess what? These are still Bible times! Jesus Christ is the same yesterday, today, and He is forever the same! What He did before, He still does today. In fact, in my own life and ministry, I have personally had well over one hundred angelic encounters where they have come and appeared to me—releasing messages, the tangible presence of God, and the empowering work of the Holy Spirit. Yes, angels are flames of fire and ministering spirits sent to assist us in our assignments in God.

Yes, God indeed created angels. Isn't it amazing to ponder on the reality that only God Himself is not a created being? God just is. Period! Lucifer, on the other hand, is a created being, originally created as an angelic prince. So God the Father and Lucifer do not even belong in the same sphere when it comes to ranks of authority, function, placement in the cosmos, origins, and life in eternity.

There are hundreds of scriptures we could dive into that confirm God created angels, but I've prayerfully selected a few of the most revealing such as Psalm 148:2–5, John 1:1–3, and Colossians 1:16. I must cite upfront extremely important Scripture verses that warn us to worship God only—not to worship angels: Revelation 22:8–9, Colossians 2:18, Luke 4:7–8, Romans 1:25, and Matthew 4:9–10. We worship *with* angels; we do not worship angels. We do not worship created beings; we worship the Creator.

Each individual angel is a marvelous, distinct, and direct creation by God the Father. God spoke and they came into being. Unlike humankind, angels do not procreate (see Matthew 22:28–30). This is a very important point to keep in mind, especially when dealing with spiritual warfare and the terrorizing activity of demonic spirits.

Two Most Asked Questions about Angels

Two pragmatic questions I am most asked about angels are, "How many angels are there?" and "When were angels created?" For the number of angels God created, let me refer you to Hebrews 12:22, which states, "But you have come to Mount Zion and to the city of the living God, the heavenly Jerusalem, and to myriads of angels." Also, a divine commentary is found in Revelation 5:11: "Then I looked, and I heard the voices of many angels around the throne and the living creatures and the elders; and the number of them was myriads of myriads, and thousands of thousands."

How many angels does *myriads* mean? The etymology or word history indicates that *myriads* comes from a Greek word that means "countless" or "ten thousand." The indication from a human perspective is that there's such a vast number of angels that they appear to be unnumberable in man's capacity to count!

The angels are not just limited to filling heaven though. They are also among us. We see this in the dream of Jacob's ladder as recorded in Genesis 28:12: "And behold, the angels of God were ascending and descending on it." They were ascending first. That means they were already here on earth.

Let's move on to the second most asked question, "When were angels created?" Like humankind, God created angels at some specific point in time. Genesis 1:16 records the fourth day of creation where God "made the stars also." Now, of course, that is a reference to the literal stars in the celestial heavenly places. But there are multiple scriptural references as "stars" also being used as a descriptive term for angels. While I believe that Genesis 1:16 is a literal reference to the stars we see at night, I will not discount the possibility that this could also include angels as some of God's bright and shining displays of His brilliant creation on the fourth day. (I will give another possible explanation to this question shortly.)

Consider with me Job 38:4–7 (NIV):

Where were you when I laid the earth's foundation? Tell me, if you understand. Who marked off its dimensions? Surely you know! Who stretched a measuring line across it? On what were its footings set, or who laid its cornerstone—while the morning stars sang together and all the angels shouted for joy?

I have written extensively on this particular subject in *Angelic Encounters* and *Angelic Encounters Today Study Guide*. Please refer to those two resources for an in-depth teaching.

Who are these heavenly beings? Different faith traditions offer a variety of perspectives. In his book *The Table-Talk of Martin Luther*, Protestant reformer Martin Luther gives us a wonderful definition of these celestial beings: "An angel is a spiritual creature created by God without a body, for the service of Christendom and of the church."[1]

Reformed theologian John Calvin wrote a lot about angels in his massive number of theological works. In *Institutes of the Christian Religion* he states, "Angels are the dispensers and administrators of the Divine beneficence towards us . . . they guard our safety, undertake our defense, direct our ways, and exercise a constant solicitude that no evil befall us."[2] That is brilliant writing, is it not?

From a historical Catholic perspective, "An angel is a pure spirit created by God. The Old Testament theology included the belief in angels: the name applied to certain spiritual beings or intelligences of heavenly residence, employed by God as the ministers of His will. . . . When we meet messengers doing supernatural things, there is no doubt they are heavenly beings—God's messengers, working for Him and for the ultimate benefit of mankind."[3]

From a Jewish theological background, Rabbi Geoffrey Dennis gives us a peek into the role of angels in Jewish tradition: "Angels can come in a wondrous variety of forms . . . . They appear humanoid in most Biblical accounts . . . but they also may manifest themselves as pillars of fire and cloud, or as a fire within a bush (Exodus 3). The Psalms characterize natural phenomenon, like lightning, as God's [angels] (Psalm 104:4). Other divine creatures appear to be winged parts of God's throne (Isaiah 6) or of the divine chariot (Ezekiel 1). The appearance of cherubim is well known enough to be artistically rendered on the Ark of the Covenant (Exodus 25). . . . Biblical angels fulfill a variety of functions, including conveying information to mortals, shielding, rescuing, and caring for Israelites, and smiting Israel's enemies."[4]

One of the greatest books I read on the topic of angels is *Angels: God's Secret Agents* by Reverend Billy Graham, the evangelical statesman of recent time. He wrote, "We find angels belong to a uniquely different dimension of creation that we, limited to the natural order, can scarcely comprehend. In this angelic domain the limitations are different from those God has imposed on the natural order. . . . They are God's messengers whose chief business is to carry out His orders in the world. He has given them an ambassadorial charge. He has designated and empowered them as holy deputies to perform works of righteousness."[5]

I am quite aware there are other views on when angels were created. Some believe angels were created very early, and thus Lucifer's fall happened in the space and time before chaos entered God's perfectly created cosmos and before the sin of Adam changed the spiritual climate of the Garden of Eden. The fall of Lucifer created disorder in the heavenly places, ushering in darkness and confusion, which some Bible commentators feel occurred between Genesis 1:1 and Genesis 1:2.

Yes, there are different views on when angels were created. Bluntly stated, I was not there. I do not know.

The Three Great Angelic Princes

The three "major" angels revealed in the Old and New Testaments are Gabriel, Michael, and Lucifer. Let's look specifically at the Scripture that mentions Lucifer created as what I call an "angelic prince." Another way of referencing these angels could be as archangels.

Lucifer is depicted as "the shining one" in Isaiah 14:12, which we've already reviewed and will look at again in the next chapter.

You may be familiar with the angel Gabriel, whose name means "God is mighty" or "a mighty one of God." Multiple verses in the Bible mention Gabriel including Daniel 8:16; 9:21 and Luke 1:19, 26.

Michael's name means "who is like God," and is mentioned in Daniel 10:13, 21; 12:1. Jude 9 is a very interesting mention of Michael, the prince or archangel. Revelation 12:7 specifically says, "And there was war in heaven, Michael and his angels waging war with the dragon."

I found it very interesting when researching that in Protestant understandings three archangels are acknowledged; but in other traditions of Christianity, there is some variance on this point. Some Catholic and Orthodox traditions teach that there could be as many as twelve archangels, and they even name them, such as Tobias and others mentioned in the book of Enoch and writings of this nature.[6]

The Authority Structure of Angels

Before Lucifer's fall, it is probable that each of the three archangels commanded one-third of the angelic host. It's very easy to reference that presumption from reading Revelation 12:4: "And his tail swept away a third of the stars of heaven and hurled them to the earth." *Stars* is a very important word because in multiple places in the Bible, *stars* is interchangeably used for angels.

Colossians 1:16 states, "For by Him all things were created, both in the heavens and on earth, visible and invisible, whether thrones, or dominions, or rulers, or authorities—all things have been created through Him and for Him." This verse describes four main orders of the invisible spiritual realm:

1. Thrones
2. Dominions—a few translations say "lordships"
3. Rulers—other translations say "principalities"
4. Authorities—other translations say "powers," which denotes the realm of authority under a prince, a ruler. Thus, rebellion began on the level of principalities.

Now let's examine what we can learn from Satan's appearances in the book of Job: "Now, there was a day when the sons of God came to present themselves before the LORD, and Satan also came among them" (Job 1:6). Job 2:1 is fascinating: "Again, there was a day when the sons of God came to present themselves before the LORD, and Satan came also among them to present himself before the LORD."

These two verses in the book of Job—1:6 and 2:1—indicate that there was a periodic assembly of the angels. We can compare this assembly to the one mentioned in Psalm 89:5–7. Why did the angels periodically assemble in heaven and present an activity report? Not only did they report, but they also received instructions and assignments. We could also compare this to Psalm 103 where the Lord's righteous benefits and deeds are listed.

The name Lucifer is used only in the King James and the New King James versions of Isaiah 14:12; other versions cite the name Satan. Every time Lucifer is named, you will see he is associated with worship. Every time the archangel Gabriel is named, he is a messenger of God associated with the delivery of messages from God. Every time the archangel Michael is named, we see him as a warrior and defender of Israel.

Angels are real and God created them for our good. But one angelic prince fell, which we'll look at next.

———— **FOR REFLECTION AND PRAYER** ————

- Before starting to read this book, what knowledge did you have about angels?
- What circumstances in your life do you feel could be the result of angel activity?

Take a moment right now to talk to God about your desire to have angelic encouragement and protection in your life. Remember, angels are available for assignment.

5

THE FALL OF LUCIFER

How did Lucifer fall? Old Testament prophets Isaiah and Ezekiel act as detailed reporters to answer this question. These holy prophets of God spoke to historical events of their day addressing real issues, while yet, as prophets do, looking beyond their own time and peering into the future, seemingly on parallel tracks. Thus, the descriptive words we will read address more than one sphere of time and space at the same time. Complicated? Yes! But not when you truly understand the nature and operation of prophetic gifting.

Isaiah and Ezekiel, and other Old Testament prophets, have helped shape our Christian New Testament beliefs about our adversary, the devil, and his beginning, present day activity, and future. Isaiah 14:12–15 gives us one look into this blatant fall and assault upon God's throne:

> "How you have fallen from heaven, you star of the morning, son of the dawn! You have been cut down to the earth, you who defeated the nations! But you said in your heart, 'I will ascend to heaven; I will raise my throne above the stars of God, and I will sit on the mount of assembly in the recesses of the north. I will ascend above

the heights of the clouds; I will make myself like the Most High.'
Nevertheless you will be brought down to Sheol, to the recesses
of the pit."

Let's look at this passage line by line for greater understanding.

- "How you have fallen from heaven." This reveals Lucifer's
  place was originally in heaven but how he was cast to
  earth when he fell or sinned against God.
- "You star of the morning." Here we find the use of the
  term *star* as it describes his created form as an angel.
- "You have been cut down to the earth." This one who was
  created by God as a bright and shining "star" in heaven
  was removed and tossed out because of his pride. Did this
  demotion change Lucifer's attitude? Not in the least! Next
  we find him proclaiming his presumed supremacy.
- "I will ascend to heaven." Although he was already in
  heaven and in one of the highest ranks among God's created order, his assertion was that he would ascend even
  higher than his God-given rank and position.
- "I will raise my throne above the stars of God." He
  wanted to exalt himself above the other archangels and
  rule over all the heavenly hosts.
- "I will sit on the mount of assembly in the recesses of the
  north." This shows his hubris and desire to rule over the
  assembly of angels, usurping God's appointment and
  assignment.
- "I will ascend above the heights of the clouds." He wanted
  to live above heaven, as being better than those who make
  heaven their home.
- "I will make myself like the Most High." This statement
  now goes to the extreme because he not only wants to be
  the chief ruler of the created order, but now also declares

that he is worthy of being on an equal plane as the One and only One who is not a created being—God Himself.

Jesus, as the eternal Son of God, witnessed the fall of Satan as recorded in Luke 10:18: "And He said to them, 'I watched Satan fall from heaven like lightning.'" The term *lightning* in Scripture is used to refer to multiple things. Job 36:32 states that God's hands are covered with glory or with lightning, and He sends it forth to strike the mark.

As discussed earlier, stars are also used as a reference to angels. Lightning is a very clear depiction of the glory realm of God. So when Lucifer, who was originally created as a majestic angel filled with the glorious, bright dimensions of God, falls, it makes sense that it came with a crash or strike of lightning. Thus Jesus could say, "I watched Satan fall from heaven like lightning."

Lucifer's Haughty Heart

Ezekiel 28:12–19 is another passage that shows us what happened with Lucifer, specifically how he became prideful and rebellious because of his beauty. Although a long portion of Scripture, I encourage you to read it carefully.

> Son of man, take up a song of mourning over the king of Tyre and say to him, "This is what the LORD God says: 'You had the seal of perfection, full of wisdom and perfect in beauty. You were in Eden, the garden of God; every precious stone was your covering: the ruby, the topaz and the diamond; the beryl, the onyx and the jasper; the lapis lazuli, the turquoise and the emerald; and the gold, the workmanship of your settings and sockets, was in you. On the day that you were created they were prepared. You were the anointed cherub who covers, and I placed you there. You were on the holy mountain of God; you walked in the midst of the stones of fire. You were blameless in your ways from the day you were created until unrighteousness was found in you. By the abundance of

your trade you were internally filled with violence, and you sinned; therefore I have cast you as profane from the mountain of God. And I have destroyed you, you covering cherub, from the midst of the stones of fire. Your heart was haughty because of your beauty; you corrupted your wisdom by reason of your splendor. I threw you to the ground; I put you before kings, that they may see you. By the multitude of your wrongdoings, in the unrighteousness of your trade you profaned your sanctuaries. Therefore I have brought fire from the midst of you; it has consumed you, and I have turned you to ashes on the earth in the eyes of all who see you. All who know you among the peoples are appalled at you; you have become terrified and you will cease to be forever.'"

Let's take time to unwrap the revelations contained in what God has to say about Lucifer throughout this passage of Scripture. First, we must distinguish between the "son of man" and the "king of Tyre." The son of man was a mortal man (verses 2 and 9), and the king was a demonic entity, a fallen angelic cherub undoubtedly Lucifer himself (verses 12–16).

In my opening comments of this chapter, I stated how the prophets often addressed multiple spheres on parallel tracks at the same time. They would often paint artistically at one moment, weave in a narrative rooted as a historian, and shift their gaze, look up and beyond, and scribe as a foreteller. Thus, three spheres appear in their literature as overlapping concentric circles: history past, history present, and history future. So we find terms, cities, and names of people interchangeably used—spiritually, naturally, historically, and future tense.

Now I also understand this dimension because this is the way some prophetic vessels operate today. This is true in the case of seer prophets in particular. C. Peter Wagner used to refer to me as the historian of the prophets. I know what it is like to start on one revelatory plane, shift into the teacher sphere, and end up in a full-blown futuristic seer realm. I trust this will help some in their interpretive skills.

Psalm 149 does this for us when verse 6 states, "The high praises of God shall be in their mouths." Then verse 8 clearly states, "To bind their kings with chains, and their dignitaries with shackles of iron." Verse 9 culminates by declaring, "To execute against them the judgment written. This is an honor for all His godly ones." Who are the kings and dignitaries verse 8 speaks of? Are they natural or spiritual? We will soon learn these terms are often used in a dual manner. Those versed in spiritual warfare understand Psalm 149 speaks of demonic territorial powers of darkness in descending ranks of authority that are subject to the praise of God's people.

With this in mind, as we look at this detailed passage in Ezekiel, we can grasp how Tyre was, and is, a literal city, and also references the king as a temporary ruling power of darkness in the heavenly places.

Let's look at this verse by verse, seeing how Ezekiel described Lucifer, the "shining star":

- Sealed with perfection, full of wisdom, perfect in beauty (12).
- Visited Eden, the garden of God (13).
- Covered with every precious stone (13).
- Created as the anointed covering cherub on God's holy mountain (14).
- Created perfect, but unrighteousness overcame him (15).
- Filled with abundance, which led to violence and sin (16).
- Cast out because of his rebellion and banished from the mountain of God or the place where He dwells (16).
- Filled with sinful pride and hubris, and his wisdom was corrupted (17).
- Possibly facing the final stage of judgment, or in the future (18).

This Scripture paints a very vivid picture of how perfect God's creation was and how Lucifer's unrighteousness caused him to be banished from his Creator's presence in the heavenly realm.

A Probable Outline of Lucifer's Rebellion

Lucifer, a created angel, became Satan, the adversary and resister, according to what God said through Ezekiel. Revelation 12:3–4 (AMP) tells us "a great fiery red dragon (Satan) . . . his tail swept [across the sky] and dragged away a third of the stars of heaven and flung them to the earth." And Revelation 12:9 (NIV) says, "The great dragon was hurled down—that ancient serpent called the devil, or Satan, who leads the whole world astray. He was hurled to the earth, and his angels with him."

When we put the details from Isaiah, Ezekiel, and Revelation together, what do we see? We see that heaven and earth were made perfect by God. God committed a special task of worship to Lucifer, an anointed covering cherub. Lucifer became proud of his own wisdom and beauty and aspired to a position equal with God. This position was occupied by the Son of God.

Lucifer systematically promoted rebellion and seduced the angels under his charge from their loyalty to God. He then led them in an assault upon God's throne. As a result of these actions, he and a third of the deceived angels that rebelled with him were cast down from the heaven of God's dwelling.

They then set up a rival kingdom in opposition to God. This false kingdom is situated in the heavenlies, but below what the Bible calls the third heaven. The first heaven is what we see with our natural eyes—clouds, sun, moon, stars. The third heaven is God's dwelling place and our eternal home. The second heaven is below God's dwelling place and above the first heaven. The second heaven, or midheaven, is Satan's domain and where spiritual warfare most often takes place.

After Satan set up his sphere of rule, he took the form of the crafty serpent and deceived Adam and Eve, who subsequently sinned and fell from their place of dominion in the garden of Eden (see Genesis 3). This is commonly referred to as the "original sin," or the first sin that affected the future of all mankind for all time.

Then the greatest war of all began.

All human beings are born in the midst of that battle between good and evil. There is no neutral ground or middle position for any of us. As people try to believe or act to the contrary, either we are on one side of this cosmic clash or the other. I repeat, therefore, what I said earlier in the section on warring kingdoms: we are born *in* war and we are born *for* war.

Pride Comes Before a Fall

We have read in Isaiah 14 the five times Lucifer promoted himself: "I will. . . . I will. . . . I will. . . . I will. . . . I will. . . ." This attitude has nothing to do with the Kingdom of God. This kind of self-promotion goes against the "others first" and servant mindset that identifies the Kingdom of God. Pride is something that we each have to deal with in our own lives, is it not?

Understanding your gifting, your calling with God, and being a pursuer of your destiny is one thing, a healthy thing. But self-promotion, self-exaltation, and hubris is another thing, and sometimes there's a very fine line between the two. Right?

That's why we need the ministry of the Holy Spirit in our lives. That's why we need to learn practical lessons about spiritual warfare. We must not compromise with a "shining one" who was created to worship God but promoted himself instead, became a deceiver, and fell from heaven.

We need to recognize where we stand—with God or with Satan. We must invite the Holy Spirit, even right now, to come and point out areas in our lives where we are self-exalting and are standing on common ground—maybe unknowingly—with the powers of darkness. We must allow the blood of Jesus to cleanse us. We are to be grateful for fresh and new opportunities each day to serve Him and others.

While we have looked at Lucifer's rebellion and his evil plans, we can say confidently that we are more than triumphant conquerors in Christ Jesus as we humbly submit to His lordship in our lives. To Him be glory and honor for every victory!

FOR REFLECTION AND PRAYER

- How did the full context of Isaiah 14, Ezekiel 28, and Revelation 12 open your eyes to what happened with Lucifer?
- Why is pride such a big deal when it comes to spiritual warfare?

VICTORIOUS SPIRITUAL WARFARE PRAYER

Heavenly Father, I am grateful that the Kingdom of God is an upside-down Kingdom, where the rule of humility and kindness wins over self-assertion and self-promotion. I come out of alignment with the five "I wills" of Lucifer, a created being, and I align myself with the Kingdom of God—the righteousness, peace, and joy in the Holy Spirit.

I am grateful for the insight You granted to me through the Word of God about the rebellion and the fall of Lucifer, a created angelic made to worship You. I repent of pride in my own life, humble myself before You, and ask for Your grace since Your Word declares that You resist the proud but give grace to the humble. I now assume my rightful place in worship and adoration, and I declare, "Worthy, worthy, worthy is the Lamb of God to receive glory and honor and majesty, both now and forevermore." Amen and amen!

THE RESULTS OF LUCIFER'S REBELLION

"You belong to your father, the devil, and you want to carry out your father's desires. He was a murderer from the beginning, not holding to the truth, for there is no truth in him. When he lies, he speaks his native language, for he is a liar and the father of lies."

John 8:44 NIV

The contrast between light and darkness has never been more distinct than when we compare the nature of the uncreated Son of God, Jesus Christ, and the nature of the fallen archangel, Lucifer, who attempted to be like the Most High God.

Jesus said, "I am the light of the world. If you follow me, you won't have to walk in darkness, because you will have the light that leads to life" (John 8:12 NLT). Jesus also said, "My light will shine for you just a little longer. Walk in the light while you can, so the darkness will not overtake you. Those who walk in the darkness cannot see where they are going" (John 12:35 NLT).

One of Satan's tactics is to keep us in the dark by trying to prevent the light of God's love from shining through. Too often we allow our day-to-day circumstances to form a dark cloud over us, keeping us right where Lucifer wants us—in darkness where he can feed us lies.

What is our defense and how will we triumph? The Word of God has our answer: Light. Psalm 18:28, 105:39, 112:4, John 1:5, John 8:12, Ephesians 5:8, 1 John 1:5, and many more "enlightening" Scriptures in God's Word make this clear. Matthew 4:16 (NLT) tells us, "The people who sat in darkness have seen a great light. And for those who lived in the land where death casts its shadow, a light has shined."

As you read the next two chapters, embrace the words of 1 John 1:5 (NLT), which says, "This is the message we heard from Jesus and now declare to you: God is light, and there is no darkness in him at all." Amen and amen!

6

THE SNARE OF PRIDE AND INSECURITY

I remember when I was new in ministry and the Holy Spirit whispered a word of wisdom to me: "Before honor comes humility." At the time I was not aware that this was a biblical phrase located in Proverbs 15:33. But nonetheless, I knew I had heard a word that cut deeply at the core of pride in my own heart, and it related to an issue of self-promotion before man in my own life and ministry at that formative period of time.

It hit home in a very personal way. So I purposed in my heart, that I would not take the lead role in our emerging Jesus People fellowship at the time, and yield the right of way to someone younger than I in age, but perhaps more advanced in the ways of God. I had to rely on the truth that "before honor comes humility." So I chose to take the secondary seat and serve another.

You know what? Even if it was the right thing to do, it still did hurt. It hurt my pride. So I swallowed hard. But when we learn that we are living our lives for Him and His ways, and not for a position before men, eventually, God's ways pay off. Pride is subtle and the Holy Spirit has a way of chipping away at it over and over again in our lives.

Humility Versus Pride

God's Kingdom is the kingdom of humility. Lucifer's is the pinnacle of pride.[1] As we looked at the passages in Isaiah and Ezekiel, we saw how Lucifer's pride caused his fall from his position in heaven. One result of his rebellion is the rampant pridefulness that instigates chaos worldwide today. Pride in a job well done can be good, but pride that makes people believe they are entitled to more than others, deserve special treatment, or demand extra privileges is not godly pride.

Lucifer's brand of pride causes wars between families, churches, organizations, communities, regions, and nations.

A spirit of humility is the opposite of pride. To walk in humility is to walk in authority and victory in spiritual warfare. A key weapon of spiritual warfare is walking in the opposite spirit of pride. When you walk in humility, you walk in the character and the nature of Christ Jesus.

James, the half-brother of Jesus, reminded the early Church, "God opposes the proud but gives grace to the humble" (James 4:6 NLT). Grace is released through humility, and the supernatural hand of God comes to fight for us. Our tendency is to want to fight for ourselves. There are times to care for personal needs, speak up, and act to protect what God has entrusted to us, but God does not want us to use carnal weapons when we do this.

Luke 14:11 (NIV) states, "For all those who exalt themselves will be humbled, and those who humble themselves will be exalted." In fact, the Scripture boldly declares that God "mocks proud mockers but shows favor to the humble and oppressed" (Proverbs 3:34 NIV).

In relation to the world's values and priorities, God's are upside-down. This is revealed in Philippians 2:5–11 (NIV) through the sacrificial life of the Lord Jesus Christ:

> In your relationships with one another, have the same mindset as Christ Jesus: Who, being in very nature God, did not consider equality with God something to be used to his own advantage;

rather, he made himself nothing by taking the very nature of a servant, being made in human likeness. And being found in appearance as a man, he humbled himself by becoming obedient to death—even death on a cross!

Therefore God exalted him to the highest place and gave him the name that is above every name, that at the name of Jesus every knee should bow, in heaven and on earth and under the earth, and every tongue acknowledge that Jesus Christ is Lord, to the glory of God the Father.

This Scripture passage is an excellent example of how humbleness results in exaltation. Jesus exhibited seven acts of humility, which were followed by seven steps of exaltation by God the Father in response.

1. Jesus did not consider equality with God. He didn't laud control over others.
2. Jesus made Himself nothing; He emptied Himself. He was filled only with love and compassion.
3. Jesus took on the form, the nature, of a servant (also see Matthew 20:28).
4. Jesus left heaven and came to earth in human likeness. He arrived as a child to a young woman.
5. Jesus looked like an ordinary man. He was a carpenter, not a king on a white horse.
6. Jesus humbled Himself. He even washed the disciples' feet.
7. Jesus was obedient to death on a cross (also see Luke 22:42). He died a criminal's death though He was without sin.

Verses 9–11 show God's response of seven acts of exaltation:

1. God exalted, or elevated, Jesus.
2. God gave Jesus the highest honor.
3. God gave Jesus the name above all other names.

4. God attached honor and glory to Jesus' name.

5. Jesus' name causes every knee to bend and praise Him.

6. Jesus will be worshiped by all in heaven, on earth, and under the earth.

7. All will declare and acknowledge that Jesus Christ is Lord, to the glory of God the Father.

We must believe and live two truths:

1. Godly character displaces the works of evil.

2. Humility displaces and destroys pride.

By walking in the opposite spirit of the world in the character and love of Jesus, we are enforcing the Kingdom of God. *Lord, please help us. Teach us these ways of Yours.*

How can we live that way? Security in Christ is the key.

Security Versus Insecurity

Another ripple effect of the result of Lucifer's rebellion is that it brought the subtle yet disastrous feelings of insecurity into the world. Countless millions of people, young and old, lack confidence, have panic attacks, and feel anxious or threatened. Our last days spiritual warfare has escalated to such a degree that we are now caught up in a suicidal generation.

We used to think that darkness lurked only in the in the alleyways and the overt dimensions of the occult. Times have changed but his methods have not. Lucifer is busy pushing his age-old, demonic, self-promotion agenda in the arts, entertainment and media, journalism, homes, and every region. He has a scheme for every country and even plots in churches.

But Jesus is always the answer, and intimacy with Him is a vital key to feeling secure enough to make a righteous stand when the battle is raging. Being triumphant in spiritual warfare starts with removing any internal common ground you may have with the enemy. Security in Jesus, knowing you are free from danger and threats, develops from intimacy with your Lord and Savior.

This is not the usual way spiritual warfare is taught. Walking in the truths Jesus shared in His Sermon on the Mount is the prerequisite to effective, long-term spiritual warfare. Typically, people are told something more like, "Call on the name of Jesus, declare the blood, and let's conquer the enemy!" But when you remove any opinions, attitudes, or interests that you may share with the enemy (like pride, ungodly ambition, and jealousy), you become more secure in your relationship with Jesus. Then you can exercise authentic authority over the devil and his schemes.

Before we engage in spiritual conflict, we must carefully consider Ephesians 1:3–14.

> Blessed be the God and Father of our Lord Jesus Christ, who has blessed us with every spiritual blessing in the heavenly places in Christ, just as He chose us in Him before the foundation of the world, that we would be holy and blameless before Him. In love He predestined us to adoption as sons and daughters through Jesus Christ to Himself, according to the good pleasure of His will, to the praise of the glory of His grace, with which He favored us in the Beloved. In Him we have redemption through His blood, the forgiveness of our wrongdoings, according to the riches of His grace which He lavished on us. In all wisdom and insight He made known to us the mystery of His will, according to His good pleasure which He set forth in Him, regarding His plan of the fullness of the times, to bring all things together in Christ, things in the heavens and things on the earth. In Him we also have obtained an inheritance, having been predestined according to the purpose of Him who works all things in accordance with the plan of His will, to the end that we who were the first to hope in the Christ would be to the praise of His glory. In Him, you also, after listening to the message of truth, the gospel of your salvation—having

also believed, you were sealed in Him with the Holy Spirit of the promise, who is a first installment of our inheritance, in regard to the redemption of God's own possession, to the praise of His glory.

Revealed in these words is God's blessing to us in the spiritual realm—His choosing and adoption of us, His pleasure, and His redemption of us. We're also told of His love lavished on us with all wisdom and understanding, His predestination and plan for us, and His sealing with the promise of the Holy Spirit.

We see that God wants us to be open to all that He pours out for us as we cry out to Him. Only then is there security for us to stand in the day of battle; otherwise, we will be tossed around by the enemy. These truths are so very important. I give you an assignment right now to pray-read—yes, pray-read—Ephesians 1. I have based my life on the foundational truths found in this apostolic epistle.

Ephesians 6 is another important pre-battle reading as Paul wrote of putting on the full armor of God, which includes the belt of truth, the body armor of righteousness, shoes of peace, the shield of faith, the helmet of salvation, and the sword of the Spirit, which is the Word of God (see Ephesians 6:13–17 NLT). We must know who we are in Christ Jesus and what He provided for us to feel and be secure in our battle stance.

God pronounced that He was pleased with His Son before He ever performed one miracle, healed the sick, preached a sermon, or cast out a demon (see Matthew 3:17; Luke 3:22). Jesus was secure in His Father's love, and that's where authentic, true spiritual warfare must be grounded.

Satan, in contrast, exerts his own will to promote himself ambitiously. He was not content in his position, function, or relationship with the Father; consequently, Satan is constantly overreaching and grappling for recognition—and we too often give it to him.

Two big results of Lucifer's sin are pride and insecurity, and pride and insecurity open the door for sin. When we put on the humility of Christ and embrace our identity in Him, we are better able to take authority over the devil and his tactics, which we will look at in the next chapter.

FOR REFLECTION AND PRAYER

- Describe the battle between humility and pride in your own life.
- When has God resisted you because of pride, and when have you experienced God's grace because you have humbled yourself?
- How is intimacy with God connected to security?

Take a few moments right now to talk to God about your desire to walk in humility, secure as His beloved child.

7

SATAN'S PLAN AND TACTICS

God has a plan for every person on earth. It is up to us to choose to follow His divine path for our lives. God tells us in the well-known verse Jeremiah 29:11, "'For I know the plans that I have for you,' declares the Lord, 'plans for prosperity and not for disaster, to give you a future and a hope.'"

This was Michal Ann's life verse. It was handwritten on a note card and was placed on the window at the kitchen sink at our farmhouse. So we saw this purpose-filled Scripture everyday. Michal Ann embodied hope, and this too is a vital weapon of spiritual warfare.

The enemy also has a plan for each person. Rather than providing a hopeful future for us, the devil's plan is to steal, kill, and destroy us (see John 10:10).

Let's make this personal: God has a wonderful plan for your life. Please absorb that truth into your spirit. Don't compare your life to someone else's life. The enemy's scheme is to keep you from appreciating the life you have. God has a distinct, tailor-made plan for your life.

I've had the honor of traveling around the world. Not many would have ever thought a skinny boy from a town of 259 people, who had fears galore, would travel the world, write more than 50 books, speak to many thousands of people, sit with kings and presidents—and still have the best years in front of me. So I want you to know this: Although the enemy has a plan, God's plan always trumps the devil's.

The Enemy's Schemes

The devil may be sinful, but he is definitely not dumb, and he does not act haphazardly without a goal in view. He is not, however, all-knowing. Paul the apostle wrote about how he had become familiar with Satan's evil schemes:

> When you forgive this man, I forgive him, too. And when I forgive whatever needs to be forgiven, I do so with Christ's authority for your benefit, so that Satan will not outsmart us. For we are familiar with his evil schemes.
>
> 2 Corinthians 2:10–11 NLT

The devil has designs and plans to outsmart us. *Outwit* is the term the New International Version uses, and the New American Standard Bible translates verse 11 like this: "so that no advantage would be taken of us by Satan." Let's not be ignorant of this tactic to cheat or defraud by deception.

Paul also uses the word *schemes*, meaning "a method" (see Ephesians 6:11). Our enemy is extremely methodical—even more than we are—in his approach. He wears us down and is cunning in his strategies. This enemy of God has a downward spiraling plan for your life, filled with evil, methodical schemes. Many believers don't understand this regarding spiritual warfare. The devil will find a gap in your armor and work methodically to squeeze sin or other weights into your life.

When the devil tempted Jesus (see Matthew 4:1–11), he used the Word of God and twisted it. Thankfully, Jesus knew the truth, so He wasn't fooled. We must know the Word of God because the enemy knows the Bible too. I wonder sometimes if the devil reads the Bible more than we do! If he twisted the Word with Jesus, of course he will do that with us.

Not only does the enemy twist the Word of God, he also works to undermine authentic, Spirit-led words we receive from others. If you've ever been given a prophetic word, do you think the enemy doesn't know it? God wants us to stand on His promises, wage war with those words, and claim our victory in Jesus' name. (You are going to love the last section of this book!)

Satan's Specific Works

Let's look at some of the works of the enemy—what has come about because of his rebellion. Paul writes in 2 Corinthians 4:3–4 (NIV):

> Even if our gospel is veiled, it is veiled to those who are perishing. The god of this age [the enemy] has blinded the minds of unbelievers, so that they cannot see the light of the gospel that displays the glory of Christ, who is the image of God.

According to 2 Corinthians 4:4, the devil works in active opposition to the Gospel of the Kingdom. When we present the Gospel, we are facing two obstacles:

1. Fleshly, sinful, self-resistance to the truth
2. Satanic, demonic hardening or blinding

We must present the truth to pierce through the lies, live our lives in Christlike character and conduct, and pray for the removal of the "blinders," which is satanic opposition. We must realize that we face supernatural opposition. We can confirm this reality with many scriptures, including Acts 13:6–12, Matthew 13:4, 19, and 1 Thessalonians 2:18. Let's look at eighteen other works of the enemy. Which of these do you see working in your life?

1. We just looked at 2 Corinthians 4:4 that says the enemy prevents people from seeing the light of the Gospel.

2. Satan can be the source of sickness (Acts 10:38 and others).

3. The enemy causes and intensifies the fear of death (Hebrews 2:14).

4. The devil plants sinful plans and purposes in people's minds (John 13:2, Acts 5:3, and others).

5. Occasionally Satan can indwell a person (John 13:27).

6. The devil sets a trap to capture people (1 Timothy 3:7; 2 Timothy 2:24–26).

7. Our enemy attempts to infiltrate the Church and plant his own people within it (Matthew 13:39). Yes, he does! He infiltrates multiple aspects of society.

8. Satan tests and tries Christians (Luke 22:31).

9. The devil incites persecution, imprisonment, and political oppression of believers (1 Peter 5:8–9; Revelation 2:10). What is going on in the world today is not new.

10. Our enemy is the accuser of believers (Revelation 12:10).

11. Satan performs false signs and wonders to deceive the naïve (Exodus 7; Matthew 4:8; 2 Thessalonians 2).

12. The enemy can kill, steal, and destroy (Job 1:13; John 10:10).

13. The devil seeks to intimidate and silence the witness of the Church (Revelation 12:10–12).

14. Satan stirs up disunity. That's a big one, isn't it—division over minor issues and making them major to sow seeds of bitterness and unforgiveness (2 Corinthians 2:10–11).

15. The enemy dispenses false doctrine. In fact, he's the originator of it (1 Timothy 4:1–3; Revelation 2:24).

16. Possibly the devil can and does at times manipulate the weather (Job 1:18–19; Mark 4).

17. Satan attempts to influence the thoughts and actions of unbelievers (Ephesians 2:1–2).

18. The devil is the tempter (1 Thessalonians 3:5).

The devil is the enemy of God and humankind. He is not equal to God in presence, function, or power exerted. The devil's judgment has been written, and he is in a hurry *trying*—that's a key word—to inflict as much punishment on the human race as possible before his time is over. Satan rules by dictatorial domination, in contrast to God's government, which is made up of volunteer servants responding freely to God's great love and servant leadership, demonstrated through Christ's substitutionary death on the cross and resurrection into new life.

I believe that Satan's rebellion was to be a lesson to the universe through all coming ages—a perpetual testimony to the nature of sin and its terrible results. The working out of Satan's rule and its effect upon both humans and angels shows the fruit of setting aside divine, holy authority.

The inhabitants of the universe, both loyal and disloyal, will one day understand that God is "the Rock! His work is perfect; for all His ways are justice, a God of truth and without injustice; righteous and upright is He" (Deuteronomy 32:4 NKJV). Amen and amen.

FOR REFLECTION AND PRAYER

- Where have you seen the enemy's plan at work in your personal life?

- Which of "Satan's specific works" do you recognize around you at this time? How have you dealt with these attacks?

Take a few moments to talk to the Lord about the attacks of the enemy you primarily see and how He wants you to triumph over each one.

VICTORIOUS SPIRITUAL WARFARE PRAYER

Almighty Father, I exalt the Lord Jesus Christ. He indeed is worthy of my praise, adoration, and worship. I'm amazed at His humility when He emptied Himself, took on the form of a servant, became an ordinary man, and lived a sinless life. He was obedient even unto death, and on the cross died the death of a criminal, which He did not deserve. But death could not hold Him.

Thank You, God, that on the third day, Jesus was raised from the dead, and You highly exalted Him and gave Him the name that is above every name in heaven, on earth, and under the earth. I fall out of agreement with the pride of Lucifer that caused him to fall from his position and assignment and lead a rebellion. I want nothing to do with Satan the liar, thief, deceiver, and murderer.

In Christ Jesus, I am on the winning side. Jesus is triumphant and has conquered Satan, death, hell, and the domain of darkness. I stand in that victory today and declare with the heavenly host, "Glory to God in the highest. Holy, holy, holy is the Lord God Almighty, who was, who is, and is to come!" Amen and amen!

WAR IN THE HEAVENLIES

And there was war in heaven, Michael and his angels waging war with the dragon. The dragon and his angels waged war, and they did not prevail, and there was no longer a place found for them in heaven.

Revelation 12:7–8

Did you know that we have some wrong beliefs concerning heaven? Some say there are no tears in heaven. That sounds good, but it is not what the Good Book actually says. It states, "[God] will wipe every tear from their eyes" (Revelation 7:17, 21:4).

Consider another insightful statement found in Revelation 12:7–8, which begins with "And there was war in heaven." This statement contradicts many people's theological beliefs because we automatically think there is only peace in heaven. But John makes it quite clear when he writes that Michael and his angels were waging war with the dragon. The dragon is Lucifer, and his fallen angels are with him in this battle.

But Evil did *not* prevail. Every battle's victory, as always, belongs to the Lord. Verse 8 in the New Living Translation says, "The dragon lost the battle, and he and his angels were forced out of heaven."

I've stated that you were born *in* war and you were born *for* war. As we begin this next section of chapters on this war in the heavenlies in detail, let's remember the ultimate good news that Jesus wins!

8

FIVE LEVELS OF SPIRITUAL CONFLICT

Have you ever gone through a day feeling sad for no apparent reason, or everything those around you are doing is irritating and you just want to get away from them? Possibly you have walked into a public place and felt a foreboding presence, or you were simply driving your car and experienced a flood of unwanted thoughts go through your mind. Or maybe you've just been going about your day and suddenly you're gripped with fear or anxiety about a relationship or upcoming event. These experiences can be symptoms of the greater spiritual conflict happening in your world.

There are different levels of spiritual conflict that you are engaged in whether you are aware of it or not. I will drive this point home once again: You were born in the midst of a cosmic war, and you were born to be an effective weapon of spiritual warfare. There are five levels of spiritual conflict that are vital for believers to understand in order to triumph in battle:

1. The conflict between God and Satan
2. The conflict between the elect angels and the fallen angels

3. The conflict between Satan and the saints
4. The conflict between Satan and the unsaved
5. The conflict between the human mind and the Holy Spirit

Let's look at each of these five conflicts a bit more.

1. The Conflict Between God and Satan

Earlier in this book we looked at passages from Genesis, Isaiah, and Ezekiel that describe the conflict between God and Satan from the beginning. Genesis 3:15 (NLT) captures God's words to the enemy after he deceived Adam and Eve: "I will cause hostility between you and the woman, and between your offspring and her offspring. He will strike your head, and you will strike his heel." There are several prophecies in this one verse, and you can see from the beginning there was strife, enmity, and conflict between good and evil.

- God delivers a prophetic word to the enemy about the hostility that will exist between the enemy and the generational lineage of human beings.
- This verse is also a prophetic word about ongoing warfare between the seed (generational line) of Satan and the seed of God.
- The "He" in this verse refers to Jesus, who would come to earth and crush evil's head.

Let's compare Hebrews 2:14 and 1 John 3:8 regarding this perpetual war between God and the devil:

Because God's children are human beings—made of flesh and blood—the Son also became flesh and blood. For only as a human being could he die, and only by dying could he break the power of the devil, who had the power of death.

Hebrews 2:14 NLT

78

But when people keep on sinning, it shows that they belong to the devil, who has been sinning since the beginning. But the Son of God came to destroy the works of the devil.

1 John 3:8 NLT

Often people wrongly assume that this cosmic spiritual conflict between God and Satan is between two enemies who are equal in power, battling it out toward some uncertain end. That's what Satan would like for you to believe. Satan's greatest weapon is deception, and the Church's greatest need is for honest, truthful discernment.

The deceiver attempts to allure us to believe a foundational lie that he even has a chance in this battle. This fallen, created being already knows he has been completely defeated by the all-knowing, all-powerful, all-present, triumphant Lord of the universe. If you have chosen to follow Jesus, you are on the winning team! Please, remember the words of Jesus on the cross of Calvary, "It is finished!"

2. The Conflict Between the Elect Angels and the Fallen Angels

If you are interested in power clashes and intense warfare, then this subject is right up your alley. Revelation 12:7 clearly describes the battle between the righteous angels and the fallen angels: "And there was war in heaven. Michael and his angels waging war with the dragon. And the dragon and his angels waged war."

For right now, however, let's put this confrontational subject on hold, as we will look later in this book at the narrative of two territorial warring angels in the book of Daniel.

3. The Conflict Between Satan and the Saints

The conflict between the enemy and the saints is both direct and indirect. Direct conflict is often a tangible encounter between an

79

intelligent evil being and a believer. This can include temptations, traps, sicknesses, and more. Indirect conflict is the inescapable conflict we all face from simply living in a fallen society and world that is under the power of the evil one with values, ideologies, and institutions that have been influenced and shaped by Satan.

First John 5:19 says, "We know that we are children of God, and that the whole world lies in the power of the evil one." That statement sums up the reality of how believers are in the world but not of the world. Remember, "The earth is the LORD's, and all its fullness" (Psalm 24:1; 1 Corinthians 10:26, 28 NKJV). We know we are children of God, but we also know that the whole world system is under the influence and control of the evil one. Is that ever the truth—and even more so as the end-time conflicts unfold.

4. The Conflict Between Satan and the Unsaved

According to 2 Corinthians 4:4 (NLT), which we previously looked at, "Satan, who is the god of this world, has blinded the minds of those who don't believe. They are unable to see the glorious light of the Good News. They don't understand this message about the glory of Christ, who is the exact likeness of God." Perhaps family members, coworkers, or neighbors are blinded by Satan. We can pray that their blinded minds open and the light of the Lord will shine brightly on them.

We see in Ephesians 2:1–2 (NIV) that the world and Satan fight against those who are not following God: "As for you, you were dead in the transgressions and sins, in which you used to live in when you followed the ways of this world and of the ruler of the kingdom of the air, the spirit who is now at work in those who are disobedient."

In Acts 26:18 (NIV) we see that Jesus saved Paul to be a part of God's plan "to open their [the unsaved Gentiles'] eyes and turn them from darkness to light, and from the power of Satan to God, so that they may receive forgiveness of sins and a place among those who are sanctified by faith in me."

We also see how the devil works against the unsaved in Ephesians 2:2 (NLT): "You used to live in sin, just like the rest of the world, obeying the devil—the commander of the powers in the unseen world. He is the spirit at work in the hearts of those who refuse to obey God." See also Colossians 1 and Matthew 13. Satan hates those made in God's image who do not yet know Him and wages war against them to keep them in darkness.

5. The Conflict Between the Human Mind and the Holy Spirit

There is a daily battle we fight between the mind and the heart. This is why Proverbs 3:5–6 says, "Trust in the Lord with all your heart and do not lean on your own understanding. In all your ways acknowledge Him, and He will make your paths straight." The Scripture does *not* say, trust in the Lord with all your *mind*.

We live in this tussle—a continuing wrestling match of which way to lean when trusting God. We all lean one way or the other, and sometimes we lean back and forth so much that we become confused. We must allow the Spirit of God dwelling within our hearts to reign over our minds.

I have spoken prophetic words over some very intellectual people. A few times in prayer I have challenged some master communicators to let the voice of their hearts speak louder than the voice of their minds. If they would intentionally open their spiritual ears to hear their heart voice, how much more effective would they be? A lot more. We must allow the Spirit of God dwelling within our hearts to reign over our unrenewed human minds.

Another Scripture that keenly shows this conflict is Galatians 5:16–23.

> But I say, walk by the Spirit, and you will not carry out the desire of the flesh. For the desire of the flesh is against the Spirit, and

the Spirit against the flesh; for these are in opposition to one another, in order to keep you from doing whatever you want. But if you are led by the Spirit, you are not under the Law. Now the deeds of the flesh are evident, which are: sexual immorality, impurity, indecent behavior, idolatry, witchcraft, hostilities, strife, jealousy, outbursts of anger, selfish ambition, dissensions, factions, envy, drunkenness, carousing, and things like these, of which I forewarn you, just as I have forewarned you, that those who practice such things will not inherit the kingdom of God. But the fruit of the Spirit is love, joy, peace, patience, kindness, goodness, faithfulness, gentleness, self-control; against such things there is no law.

Romans also has a lot to say about this conflict:

I find then the principle that evil is present in me, the one who wants to do good. For I joyfully agree with the law of God in the inner person, but I see a different law in the parts of my body waging war against the law of my mind, and making me a prisoner of the law of sin, the law which is in my body's parts. Wretched man that I am! Who will set me free from the body of this death? Thanks be to God through Jesus Christ our Lord! So then, on the one hand I myself with my mind am serving the law of God, but on the other, with my flesh the law of sin.

Romans 7:21–25

So then, brothers and sisters, we are under obligation, not to the flesh, to live according to the flesh—for if you are living in accord with the flesh, you are going to die; but if by the Spirit you are putting to death the deeds of the body, you will live. For all who are being led by the Spirit of God, these are sons and daughters of God. For you have not received a spirit of slavery leading to fear again, but you have received a spirit of adoption as sons and daughters by which we cry out, "Abba! Father!"

Romans 8:12–15

I trust you can see more clearly that you have been born into a very real conflict, but also that you were born on the winning side. Knowing this from the beginning changes everything. Perspective changes everything!

Speaking candidly, however, sometimes it does feel like you are in the midst of a very direct demonic attack. Sometimes it can get rather challenging, thus the need for discernment on which battles are yours, and which belong to someone else to fight.

Understanding these five levels of spiritual conflict will certainly help you to fight the right conflict with the right effective weapons so you can triumph over the enemy. Can I get an amen?

FOR REFLECTION AND PRAYER

- Which of the five levels of spiritual conflict do you think has the most direct impact on your everyday life? Why?
- Which area of conflict are you the most aware of, and which are you least familiar with? What aspects of this conflict give you comfort or cause you to become fearful?
- In which area do you want to increase your wisdom to deal with spiritual conflict?

Take a few moments right now to ask the Holy Spirit to give you wisdom to discern a spiritual conflict you are facing today.

9

The Hierarchy of Satan's Dominion

Satan rules a false kingdom that is in total opposition to God. Satan also has legitimate authority over all those who are outside of God's Kingdom—those who are disobedient to God according to Ephesians 2:2 (NLT), which says, "You used to live in sin, just like the rest of the world, obeying the devil—the commander of the powers in the unseen world. He is the spirit at work in the hearts of those who refuse to obey God."

Jesus provided insight into Satan's kingdom as found in Matthew 12:25–26 (NIV):

Jesus knew their thoughts and said to them, "Every kingdom divided against itself will be ruined, and every city or household divided against itself will not stand. If Satan drives out Satan, he is divided against himself. How then can his kingdom stand? And if I drive out demons by Beelzebul, by whom do your people drive them out? So then, they will be your judges. But if it is by the Spirit of God that I drive out demons, then the kingdom of God has come upon you."

The King James and New King James translations of the Bible use the word *Beelzebub* rather than Satan, which means, "Lord of the flies" that rules the demons—the instruments of his anti-God purposes on earth.

Thank God that through Jesus' intervention, we can be delivered from Satan's authority and transferred into the Kingdom of Christ. But outside of Christ—this is an important statement—there is a system of darkness directed from the heavenlies to dominate the world system. Let's explore that some more.

More Than One Heaven

The Bible reveals that there are three different dimensions of the heavens, which I mentioned briefly in chapter 5 but will explain more in depth here:

1. The visible or first heaven with the sun, the moon, the stars, and the immediate atmosphere surrounding the earth.
2. The midheaven, as Scripture refers to it, or the second heaven, where territorial spirits of darkness temporarily rule.
3. The third heaven of God's throne and His dwelling place.

When people speak of going to heaven, they are most often referring to the third heaven where God dwells. According to the book of Job, Satan had access to the presence of God in the third heaven.

> Now there was a day when the sons [commonly understood as angels] of God came to present themselves before the LORD, and Satan also came among them. The LORD said to Satan, "From where do you come?" Satan answered the Lord and said, "From roaming about on the earth and walking around on it."
>
> Job 1:6–7

Again, there was a day when the sons of God came to present themselves before the LORD, and Satan also came among them to present himself before the LORD.

Job 2:1

Some interpretations of Revelation 12:10 state that the adversary still has temporary access to heaven, in the sense that he continually accuses believers before the throne of God:

Then I heard a loud voice in heaven, saying, "Now the salvation, and the power, and the kingdom of our God and the authority of His Christ have come, for the accuser of our brothers and sisters has been thrown down, the one who accuses them before our God day and night."

In reference to creation, Scripture refers to the "heavens," plural, and the "earth," singular. Genesis 1:1 declares, "In the beginning God created the heavens and the earth." The word for "heavens" is the Hebrew word *shamayim*, which is plural and indicates more than one heaven. Ephesians 4:10 says, "He who descended is Himself also He who ascended far above *all the heavens*, so that He might fill all things" (emphasis added). The King James Version of Ephesians 6:12 cites "high places," and is elsewhere termed "heavenly places." Ephesians 1:3, 1:20, 2:6, and 3:10 also refer to more than one heaven.

The existence of a third heaven is clearly revealed in Hebrews 12:22–24 (NLT).

But you have come to Mount Zion, to the city of the living God, the heavenly Jerusalem, and to countless thousands of angels in a joyful gathering. You have come to the assembly of God's first-born children, whose names are written in heaven. You have come to God himself, who is the judge over all things. You have come to the spirits of the righteous ones in heaven who have now been made perfect. You have come to Jesus, the one who mediates the new covenant between God and people, and to the sprinkled blood, which speaks of forgiveness instead of crying out for vengeance like the blood of Abel.

This is the third heaven, the highest heaven, where Jesus resides. The apostle Paul's reference to a third heaven is found in 2 Corinthians 12:2:

> I know a man in Christ, who fourteen years ago—whether in the body I do not know, or out of the body I do not know, God knows—such a man was caught up to the third heaven.

Paul handled revelation with the fear of the Lord, not boasting or moving into self-exaltation. Paul was humble, not even naming himself as the "man in Christ" who had this encounter in the third heaven.

Technically, the word "second heaven" is not used anywhere in the Bible, but "midheaven" is used in Revelation 14:6.

> And I saw another angel flying in midheaven with an eternal gospel to preach to those who live on the earth, and to every nation, tribe, language, and people.

The second heaven is therefore the battleground of spiritual warfare—where the war in the heavenlies takes place. (See more about the heavens in my book *The Seer*, regarding dreams, visions, and open heavens.)

Now let's turn the corner and take a look at the hierarchy of Satan's domain, namely spiritual strongholds and forces.

Spiritual Strongholds and Forces[1]

I have shared that the enemy does not work haphazardly. He has schemes, plans, and goals, with strategies and methods to carry them out. The apostle John wrote that "the whole world lies in the power of the evil one" (1 John 5:19).

One of the strategies of the enemy is to create spiritual strongholds in people's lives. A spiritual stronghold, as defined by one of my spiritual mentors Ed Silvoso, is "a mindset impregnated with hopelessness that forces you to accept as unchangeable situations or outcomes that you know are contrary to the will of God."[2] Pause. I believe that Dr. Silvoso does us a great favor in stating this one-sentence definition because we can so often over-spiritualize what a stronghold is.

Yes, there are strongholds of the mind, and there are also strongholds and spiritual forces of darkness located in the midheavens. Which do we fight? I have learned that when we discern a power of darkness, a stronghold, or a spiritual force of wickedness, we must deal with it in our own lives first.

Jesus stated, "The ruler of this world is coming, and he has nothing in Me" (John 14:30 NKJV). What does this mean? Let me share a key. We must remove the internal common ground we have with the enemy or powers of darkness we discern.

For example, if we discern a stronghold or spirit of greed in our city, in an organization, or within the culture, we must deal ruthlessly with any greed in our own hearts first. When we receive forgiveness, cleansing, healing, and deliverance over our own domain, our own lives, and our own generational iniquities, then we will have actualized authority over the *external* strongholds or forces of darkness in the heavenly places.

Six Classes of Spiritual Forces

When examining this war in the heavenlies, it is vital to know and understand six classes of spiritual forces that are battling against each other.

1. Principalities and rulers. The Hebrew word for principality, rule, power is *arche* (*Strong's* #746). A ruler must have someone, something, somewhere over which to exercise dominion or rule. The following verses in Ephesians and Colossians give us a clear description of principalities and rulers.

- ". . . far above all rule and authority, power and dominion, and every name that is invoked, not only in the present age but also in the one to come" (Ephesians 1:21 NIV).
- "His intent was that now, through the church, the manifold wisdom of God should be made known to the rulers and authorities in the heavenly realms" (Ephesians 3:10 NIV).
- "For our struggle is not against flesh and blood, but against the rulers, against the authorities, against the powers of this dark world and against the spiritual forces of evil in the heavenly realms" (Ephesians 6:12).
- "For by Him all things were created, both in the heavens and on earth, visible and invisible, whether thrones, or dominions, or rulers, or authorities—all things have been created through Him and for Him" (Colossians 1:16).

2. **Authorities.** The Greek word for authority is *exousia* (*Strong's* #1849), which demands a subordinate. The same verses above from Ephesians and Colossians apply to authorities.

3. **Powers.** Most believers know the word *dunamis* (*Strong's* #1411) as used in Ephesians 1:21. *Dunamis* means "power." Possibly some demons are stronger and thus more powerful than others. If these powers have a hierarchy or differentiation based on spiritual strength, a different and more dominant level of spiritual force is required to come against them to displace them.

4. **Dominions.** Dominion is lordship. God raised Jesus from the dead and seated Him in the heavenly places—far above all of Satan's rule, authority, power, and dominion (see Ephesians 1:20–21 and Colossians 1:16).

5. **Thrones.** We often think about thrones as referring only to God the Father Almighty's throne—of Him sitting on the

throne in heaven. While that's true, I believe there is more than one throne. How about Psalm 22:3, which says that God is "enthroned upon the praises of Israel"? Let's look at Daniel 7:9 (NLT), which says, "I watched as thrones were put in place and the Ancient One sat down to judge. His clothing was as white as snow, his hair like purest wool. He sat on a fiery throne with wheels of blazing fire."[3] So, there are thrones set up not only for God, but also for powers.

6. **World rulers.** The Greek word for a ruler of this world is kosmokrator (*Strong's* #2888) and is used only in Ephesians 6:12. God is the World Ruler. The problem is that Satan replicates that position throughout the earth through world systems such as communism and secularism. Humanism is one of the strongest end-time forms of an anti-Christ system that elevates man. In the Bible this system is identified by the number 666.

The number 6 represents man since God created man on the sixth day, so the anti-Christ as identified by the number 666 is the exaltation of humans that say, "I can do it," displacing the need for a savior—the Savior. A very real and dangerous enemy is humanism—the worship of self.

Where Are These Forces?

Ephesians 6:12 helps clarify the discussion on this hot topic of where these forces are located. Paul clearly stated that these forces of evil operate "in the heavenly realms." Some leaders use the term *territorial spirits* to describe these forces and their domain of authority. From my understanding, a territorial spirit is a demonic force operating in the midheavens but over a geopolitical sphere on a specific region on the earth (we will look at territorial spirits more in depth later in the book).

Ephesians 6:12 tells us more about where these forces are and how we are to respond. Let's look at a few different translations and see what they reveal:

- Both the New American Standard Bible and New International Version reveal these spiritual forces are in heavenly places or heavenly realms.
- The Living Bible emphasizes the active fight we are in. Passivity doesn't work! "For we are not fighting against people made of flesh and blood, but against persons without bodies—the evil rulers of the unseen world, those mighty satanic beings and great evil princes of darkness who rule this world; and against huge numbers of wicked spirits in the spirit world."
- The Amplified Version highlights the idea I have shared that we are born in war and we are born for war: "For our struggle is not against flesh and blood [contending only with physical opponents], but against the rulers, against the powers, against the world forces of this [present] darkness, against the spiritual forces of wickedness in the heavenly (supernatural) places."

Demons differ according to sinfulness (see Matthew 12:45) and also according to strength (see Mark 9:29). Could this be what determines their organizational position? Well, that isn't what really matters, is it? What matters is *your* position. Your and my position is determined by what Jesus has done on the cross for us.

Ephesians 2:6–7 says that God has "raised us up with Him, and seated us with Him in the heavenly places in Christ Jesus, so that in the ages to come He might show the boundless riches of His grace in kindness toward us in Christ Jesus." This is good news! With that in mind, let's reflect and praise Him, pausing right now as an act of worship and warfare, to exalt the triumphant name of the Lord Jesus Christ.

—— FOR REFLECTION AND PRAYER ——

- How does understanding that there are three heavens and different classes of spiritual forces help you in spiritual warfare?
- Thinking about Ed Silvoso's definition of a spiritual stronghold, can you identify "a mindset impregnated with hopelessness that causes us to accept as unchangeable situations that we know are contrary to the will of God"[4] in your own life?
- How often do you sense that something isn't right? How do you normally respond?

Take a few moments right now to talk to God about any stronghold you recognize operating in your life or in the life of someone you care about.

VICTORIOUS SPIRITUAL WARFARE PRAYER

Jesus, there is no one like You. You are the Son of God, the Son of David, the Messiah, the Prince of Peace, and the soon returning King of kings. Praise You, Lord! According to Ephesians 6:12, I declare that my wrestling match is not against flesh and blood, but against demonic rulers with descending ranks of authority, against the world dominators of this temporary present darkness, and against spiritual forces of wickedness in the heavenly places.

I joyfully submit to Your lordship in my life as I engage in this spiritual war in the heavenlies. I desire to commune with You and grow in effective spiritual warfare. I welcome the angelic hosts to come and assist me in my heavenly mandate to call forth, "Your Kingdom come on earth as it is in heaven." Amen and amen!

PART 2

OUR SPIRITUAL
WEAPONS

CHRIST'S TRIUMPH—THE DEVIL'S DEFEAT

The Son of God appeared for this purpose, to destroy the works of the devil.

1 John 3:8

The Bible is clear: Jesus came to earth to destroy the works of the devil. The key to the believer's triumph in spiritual warfare is knowing what Jesus Christ has already accomplished through His life, ministry, death, and resurrection. Jesus invites us to pray *from* a victorious mindset, not work our way *toward* one.

Christians too often live in fear of what they think the devil might do but can't, and in ignorance of what they themselves can do but don't. It is critical that every believer reckons with the reality of Christ's enthronement, the devil's dethronement, and our position in the heavenly places with Christ at the Father's right hand.

Let's look at 1 John 3:8 again: "The Son of God appeared for this purpose, to destroy the works of the devil." Notice that the word *works* is plural. We know that the devil is cunning in his goal to claim victory over the Lord's Kingdom. The word *destroy* means to crush and ruin, but it also means to loosen, unwind, unravel, or dissolve. It doesn't just mean to annihilate. Sometimes we just want to get a big hammer and bash the devil on the head, but we actually need to loosen, unwind, unravel, and dissolve him.

Bible scholar Stephen S. Smalley states that Jesus "was concerned with unpicking the net of evil in which the devil has always attempted to trap human beings."[1] That's extraordinary. Do you get it? The enemy casts a "net of evil" that traps people.

What are Satan's works? Morally, the devil entices us to sin. Physically, the devil inflicts disease. Intellectually, the devil introduces error. Spiritually, the devil blinds the minds of unbelievers, lest they see and believe the Gospel of the Kingdom.

What, then, did Jesus destroy? The verse doesn't say Jesus came to earth to destroy the devil; it says He came to destroy the *works* of the devil. Don't miss this strategic point: Jesus came to unravel the net that people get caught in. Yes, let's Praise the Lord!

HOW JESUS DESTROYED THE DEVIL'S WORKS

Throughout each person's life, there are "defining moments." I have had several, including one during my college years. It was the height of the Jesus People Movement. I might have already graduated from college—let's say it's 1974. Strait-laced Jim Goll hitchhiked from Warrensburg, Missouri, to a Presbyterian church at 55th and Oak in Kansas City where an informal, contemporary fellowship met on Sunday evenings. All of it was fascinating— the worship, Jesus people, youthful leaders, the teachers, and the hippies who were still hippies, the ex-druggies, the truth seekers, and the move of the Holy Spirit in the midst of a cultural revolution. As I recall, some were saved, some not, and some were in the process.

I sat toward the back on a hard, wooden pew. Derek Prince spoke—a British scholar who was now a profound Bible teacher of teachers of what became known globally as the charismatic movement. At some point during his presentation, he said a statement that was like an arrow that went straight into my heart: "The way of the cross leads home." I don't know if I heard anything else this distinguished man said because those words pierced me.

I already knew the Lord Jesus and was passionately on fire for Him, but that statement went into me like "well-driven nails" (see Ecclesiastes 12:11). That night, after hearing those words, I was introduced to God as Father Almighty, the Maker of heaven and earth, in an amazing, approachable way. Why? Because "the way of the cross leads home." This defining moment was a victory and what the Holy Spirit used to destroy the works of the enemy in my own personal life.

I knew Jesus as my loving Savior, Lord, and dearest Friend. But God the Father had appeared as a rather austere, aloof Man in the sky sitting on a lofty throne who seemed to hold me at arm's distance. But I was being brought to a place called home? This concept of Father God being safe, providing a safe place, and creating a place called home for me through Jesus dissolved my fears. While sitting under the authority of the apostolic teaching of the Word of God through Derek Prince, I was sovereignly delivered from the spirt of rejection, fear of man, and suicidal wishes.

I sat there and literally trembled under the authority of the Word of God, and by the end of that message I was set free. The works of the devil were exposed by the light of God's Word, and the darkness of the orphan spirit had to flee. I learned the truth and the truth set me free. Darkness lost its grip on me and everything that had a name other than the name of Jesus had to bow. This happened for me those many years ago. And it can happen for you! Jesus is still destroying the nets and the networks of the devil!

How Did Jesus Destroy the Devil's Works?

Jesus came to destroy all the works of the devil. How did He do this? First, by coming to earth! His presence on earth changed everything. His life and ministry were God's ultimate gift to the world by revealing the heavenly Father. We can see from Matthew 2 how the devil used King Herod, ruler of Jerusalem, to try to murder Jesus while He was a baby. But angels guided Jesus' father, Joseph, to escape these plots and keep Jesus safe.

Jesus also destroyed the works of the devil by living God's Word: He used the Word and relied on the Word. When the devil tempted Jesus after His forty days of fasting in the wilderness, He responded, "It is written," and quoted Scripture to refute the lies of Satan and overcome his temptations (see Matthew 4:1–11). He relied totally on God, never depending solely on His own strength or efforts.

One of the reasons we don't win all our rounds of battle is because we don't know the Word of God well enough. We don't know how to pull out the sword of the Spirit, which is the Word of God, and use it to destroy the enemy's tactics (see Ephesians 6:17). We can say, "I rebuke you, devil," but we don't know how to counter with the living words from Scripture.

Another way Jesus overcame and destroyed the works of the devil was through casting out demons and destroying spiritual strongholds, which was about one-third of Jesus' public ministry.[1] Luke 11:21–22 says,

> When a strong man, fully armed, guards his own house, his possessions are secure. But when someone stronger than he attacks him and overpowers him, that man takes away his armor on which he had relied and distributes his plunder.

Satan is the "strong man." His house, palace, or home is this present evil age. His "property" is men and women under his influence (see 2 Timothy 2). With the coming of Jesus, the Kingdom of God has arrived and has invaded the kingdom of darkness. The devil's power has been broken and his captives set free. This is just part of Christ's triumph.

The Glory of the Cross

Insofar as the cross of Christ glorified God, it also defeated Satan. How did the cross glorify the Father? Wow, that question could be answered with an entire Bible study (see John 12:23–33, Romans 3:21–26, and so much more). In his magnificent book *The Pleasures of God*, John Piper says,

> Therefore all His pain and shame and humiliation and dishonor served to magnify the Father's glory because they showed how infinitely valuable God's glory is, that such a loss should be suffered to demonstrate its worth. When we look at the racking pain and death of the perfectly innocent and infinitely worthy Son of God on the cross and hear that He endured it all so that the glory of His father, desecrated by sinners, might be restored, then we know that God has not denied the value of His own glory. . . . He has not been untrue to Himself. He has not ceased to uphold His honor and display His glory. He's just, and the justifier of the ungodly.[2]

Jesus received God's judgment against sin—against what belittled God's glory. Jesus came to vindicate and spread God's glory worldwide.

Satan seeks to keep men and women living in their sin, under its penalty, held in bondage to its power, and suffering mental and emotional defeat from its guilty accusations. Christ's death on the cross secured redemption from sin and its guilt and destroyed the devil's works (see Colossians 2:13–15).

As long as Satan can keep people in their sin, he can torment them with the fear of death—for that is sin's penalty. Let's look at Hebrews 2:14–15 (NLT):

> Because God's children are human beings—made of flesh and blood—the Son also became flesh and blood. For only as a human being could he die, and only by dying could he break the power of

the devil, who had the power of death. Only in this way could he set free all who have lived their lives as slaves to the fear of dying.

Wow! You can be set free from the fear of dying if you're in Christ Jesus. Satan persuaded Adam and Eve to turn away from God's loving guidance in the Garden and death entered the world through sin. The devil now possesses the ability to instill the fear of death in the hearts of men and women, terrorizing them with the prospect of what it will bring. But fear is destroyed through the work of the cross! Amen!

We can see in 1 Corinthians 15:50–57 how the death of Christ defeated the penalty of sin—eternal death.

> Now I say this, brothers and sisters, that flesh and blood cannot inherit the kingdom of God; nor does the perishable inherit the imperishable. Behold, I am telling you a mystery; we will not all sleep, but we will all be changed, in a moment, in the twinkling of an eye, at the last trumpet; for the trumpet will sound, and the dead will be raised imperishable, and we will be changed. For this perishable must put on the imperishable, and this mortal must put on immortality. But when this perishable puts on the imperishable, and this mortal puts on immortality, then will come about the saying that is written: "Death has been swallowed up in victory. Where, O Death, is your victory? Where, O Death, is your sting?" The sting of death is sin, and the power of sin is the Law; but thanks be to God, who gives us the victory through our Lord Jesus Christ.

Glory be to the One who removed the sting of eternal death so we can live with Christ forever.

Jesus' Resurrection and His Exaltation

As powerful as the death of Christ was, His resurrection is what gives us eternal hope. By raising Jesus from the dead and exalting

Him to sit at the right hand of God the Father, He ratified, confirmed, and openly proclaimed the sufficiency of the cross.

There are many scriptures about Christ's triumph, including:

- We are reconciled to God by the death of His Son (Romans 5:1–11).
- God raised Christ from the dead so we all can be raised when He returns to reign on the earth (1 Corinthians 15).
- The surpassing greatness of God's power raised Jesus from the dead and seated Him in the heavenly realms (Ephesians 1:19–23).
- Revelation 1:17–18 declares these glorious words of the risen Christ: "I was dead, and behold, I am alive forevermore, and I have the keys of death and Hades."

As we next examine all that Christ accomplished at the cross, I want you to know that there is always a place at the Father's table for you. Jesus' cross has made a place called home that you can inhabit and enjoy. Just as I had a defining moment in my life when I heard Derek Prince declare, "The way of the cross leads home," I now declare to you, "Because of work of the cross of Christ Jesus, there is a place setting with your name reserved at the Father's table. No one can take your place. You are special to God the Father because the way of the cross leads home!"

Now that revelation, that understanding, that declaration of truth, will destroy the works of the devil in your life like it did in mine!

FOR REFLECTION AND PRAYER

- What defining moment in your life has brought a new level of victory against the enemy?

- How often do you use Scripture to combat the enemy, and how effective is this strategy in your life when you use it?
- What is your favorite song that proclaims Jesus' victory over the enemy? What stirs in your spirit while hearing or singing the lyrics?

Take a Scripture that is close to your heart right now and turn that into a prayer of triumph that destroys the devil's works in your life.

11

THE DIVINE EXCHANGE AT THE CROSS

The cross has become a common symbol in today's culture. You see crosses on churches, on necklaces or earrings for both men and women, on bumper stickers, in media, and more. Some choose to wear a cross as jewelry even if they do not practice the Christian faith. Sadly, some don't even know that the cross is connected to Christ. But for those of us who wear a cross, see a cross on a church building, or know that Jesus died on the cross, do we know the fullness of what Christ accomplished on that old rugged cross?

If I take this further, some still carry an emblem of Christ as being crucified on the cross and have no teaching, understanding, or revelation that He was crucified, dead, and buried, and on the third day rose from the dead! I understand honoring what Jesus did on the cross. But the entire Christian faith is based on the reality that He did not remain on the cross. In fact, He did not remain in a tomb. He is risen! He is risen indeed!

When Jesus cried out, "It is finished!" what did He finish? If you said, "He paid the penalty for my sins," you would be correct. But

Jesus did so much more than that, and He wants you to receive a fresh revelation of the cross so you can receive the full benefits of what many Bible teachers and commentators have called the "divine exchange."

I personally benefited and gleaned from the many teachings I received early on from Derek Prince. There are eight aspects of the exchange made at the cross. These truths are foundational and yet revelatory at the same time. Let's take a look at them:

1. Our punishment for His peace
2. Our sorrows for His healing
3. Our sin for His righteousness
4. Our sickness for His health
5. Our curse for His blessings, goodness, mercy
6. Our poverty for His wealth
7. Our human nature for His spiritual nature
8. Our death for His life

This is glorious! Someone needs to stand up and shout for joy! Let's look at each of these eight aspects more closely. Read carefully and feel the weight of what Jesus did out of His great love for you.

1. Our Punishment for His Peace

> He was wounded for our transgressions, he was bruised for our iniquities: the chastisement [punishment] of our peace was upon him (Isaiah 53:5 KJV).

Jesus received the punishment that was due us for our sinful acts so that we may receive His peace, forgiveness, and reconciliation with the Father. Because of the cross, we can receive His peace. Wow.

2. Our Sorrows for His Healing

Surely He has borne our griefs [sicknesses] and carried our sorrows
. . . and by His stripes [wounds] we are healed (Isaiah 53:4–5 NKJV).

Jesus took upon His own body our pains and sicknesses so we
may receive healing. This truth is also quoted in the New Testament (see Matthew 8:17; Hebrews 9:28). In the spiritual realm
Jesus exchanged His peace for our transgressions and iniquities.
In the physical realm Jesus exchanged His health and healing for
our pain and sickness.

3. Our Sin for His Righteousness

Thou shalt make his soul an offering for sin (Isaiah 53:10 KJV).

Jesus exchanged His sinlessness for humankind's sinfulness. The
sin offering was identified with the sin of the one who offered it.
According to 2 Corinthians 5:21 (NIV), "God made him [Jesus]
who had no sin to be sin for us, so that in him we might become
the righteousness of God." Compare this verse to John 3 and
Numbers 21.

And how about 1 John 1:8–10: "If we say that we have no sin,
we are deceiving ourselves and the truth is not in us. If we confess
our sins, He is faithful and righteous, so that He will forgive us
our sins and cleanse us from all unrighteousness. If we say that
we have not sinned, we make Him a liar and His word is not in
us." Note the difference between *sin* (singular) and *sins* (plural)
in this passage. The sinful nature produces sinful acts, and Jesus
has carried it all.

4. Our Sickness for His Health

But it was the LORD's good plan to crush him [Jesus] and cause
him grief [including sickness]. Yet when his life is made an offering

for sin, he will have many descendants. He will enjoy a long life, and the LORD's good plan will prosper in his hands (Isaiah 53:10 NLT).

According to Micah 6:13 (NKJV), "Therefore I will also make you sick by striking you, by making you desolate because of your sins." What? This is God the Father talking about His Son. Jesus was made sick with our sickness so we may be made whole with His health.

In Acts 3:16 we see how faith in the name of Jesus provides "perfect soundness." How about 3 John 2, which shows the physical provision of God for the believer: "To be in health, even as our soul prospers."

Isaiah 52 is another example of the extreme physical sufferings of Jesus. On the cross Jesus identified with our rebellion and bore the consequences of our sin. His subsequent exaltation and the benefits of His death were made available to all people. Thank you, precious Lord Jesus!

5. Our Curse for His Blessings, Goodness, Mercy

But those who depend on the law to make them right with God are under his curse, for the Scriptures say, "Cursed is everyone who does not observe and obey all the commands that are written in God's Book of the Law." So it is clear that no one can be made right with God by trying to keep the law. For the Scriptures say, "It is through faith that a righteous person has life." This way of faith is very different from the way of law, which says, "It is through obeying the law that a person has life." But Christ has rescued us from the curse pronounced by the law. When he was hung on the cross, he took upon himself the curse for our wrongdoing. For it is written in the Scriptures, "Cursed is everyone who is hung on a tree" (Galatians 3:10–13 NLT).

Jesus took the curse that was due each one of us for breaking God's law. We in turn receive His abundant blessings by faith, which have come through the power of Christ's obedience done on our behalf.

Those who depend on their outward observance of the law to make them righteous are still under a curse. It is only through faith in Christ that we can be rescued from the curse for our self-righteousness. Much of the Body of Christ still needs a revelation of this marvelous truth concerning grace versus works. It is through faith and faith alone that we can receive the blessings of life in Christ.

According to Deuteronomy 28, these blessings are fruitfulness, abundance, protection, direction, victory, success, holiness, honor, riches, and dominion. Many Christians sometimes are enduring something they do not need to carry when they could be enjoying a blessing. If we walk in obedience, "All these blessings," it says, "shall come upon you and overtake you" (verse 2 NKJV).

And how about the blessings the psalmist sung about? Psalm 23:3, 6 (NKJV) says, "He leads me in the paths of righteousness . . . goodness and mercy shall follow me." God wants goodness and mercy to follow you and be your traveling companions!

Deuteronomy 28 also speaks of curses that can follow us. But those are the curses Jesus exchanged at the cross for us: unfruitfulness, insufficiency, frustration, failure, defeat, bondage, poverty, fear, and every form of sickness, both mental and physical.

6. Our Poverty for His Wealth

For you know the grace of Lord Jesus Christ, that though he was rich, yet for your sake he became poor, so that you through his poverty might become rich (2 Corinthians 8:9 NIV).

Jesus was made poor with our poverty so that we might be made rich with His wealth. Grace has one channel, Jesus Christ; one basis, the cross; and one Administrator, the Holy Spirit. I'm very grateful for that exchange.

Second Corinthians 9:8 (NKJV, emphasis added) reads, "God is able to make *all* grace abound toward you, that you, *always* having *all* sufficiency in *all* things, may have an abundance for every good work." I love this! Look at the many *alls* throughout this verse. What a marvelous exchange! Jesus "impoverished himself" (TPT) so we could receive God's lavish abundance.

7. Our Human Nature for His Spiritual Nature

We know that our old self was crucified with him so that the body ruled by sin might be done away with, that we should no longer be slaves to sin (Romans 6:6 NIV).

The exchange between the old and the new self is one we can enjoy immediately upon receiving Christ as Savior and Lord. The old self denotes the nature each of us received by inheritance from Adam. Our old self has been crucified with Him. Ephesians 2:2–3 (NLT) tells us, "All of us used to live that way, following the passionate desires and inclinations of our sinful nature. By our very nature we were subject to God's anger, just like everyone else."

The apostle Paul writes in Galatians 2:20 (NLT), "My old self has been crucified with Christ. It is no longer I who live, but Christ lives in me. So I live in this earthly body by trusting in the Son of God, who loved me and gave himself for me." That is true for you too.

8. Our Death for His Life

Yes, by God's grace, Jesus tasted death for everyone (Hebrews 2:9 NLT).

Jesus tasted death in three consecutive phases.

- 1. He was cut off from union and fellowship with His Father (see Habakkuk 1:3; Isaiah 59:1–2; Matthew 27:46; John 6:57, 10:30).
- 2. Jesus experienced physical death (see Matthew 27:50; Revelation 1:18).
- 3. He was banished from God's presence (see Leviticus 16:22; Psalm 16:8–11, 71:20–21, 88; Acts 2:25–31; Ephesians 4:9; 1 Peter 3:18–19).

In exchange for Jesus' gruesome death on the cross, the gift of God to believers is life in three phases:

- 1. Union and fellowship with God and being united in spirit with the Lord (see Romans 6:3–5; 1 Corinthians 6:17).
- 2. Physical life—at this time, resurrection life in our mortal body (see Romans 8:11 and 2 Corinthians 4:10–11) and after the resurrection an immortal body (see 1 Corinthians 15:51–54).
- 3. Eternity in God's presence. 1 Thessalonians 4:17 (KJV) says, "and so shall we ever be with the Lord." And compare this passage with Revelation 21:1–5.

May we never become overly familiar with any of these divine exchanges, but rather have hearts full of awe and gratitude for the eternal benefits we have because of what Jesus provided through His sacrifice. Thank you, Jesus!

--------- **FOR REFLECTION AND PRAYER** ---------

- Which of the eight aspects of the divine exchange is most familiar to you? Which had you not considered as deeply before?

- When you consider the life that Jesus offers you today (not just after you die), what kind of union and fellowship with God do you desire? What does that look like in everyday living?

Take a few moments right now to talk to God about the aspect of the cross that you are hungry for in your life right now.

12

THE DEVIL'S POSITION CHANGED BY THE CROSS

As we saw in the previous chapter, the divine exchange has produced many extraordinary benefits for each one of us. It is now possible for every person to receive forgiveness, be clothed in righteousness, and enter into fellowship and favor with God. But what Jesus did on the cross also affected the function and future of the devil. When people accept the free gift of salvation through faith in Jesus, Satan is deprived of his most sinister weapons against us. What are some of those primary weapons? Blame, shame, and guilt.

Because of the completed work of the cross, Satan's position changed, and he no longer has the authority to put blame, shame, or guilt on those who repent and put their faith in Jesus Christ.

When it comes to guilt, any person can experience true or real guilt, false guilt, and even blown-up exaggerated guilt. The blood of Jesus is the cure for every form of guilt. Remember, you shall know the truth and the truth shall set you free. This truth is huge, friend! Darkness loves to keep people uneducated, underdeveloped, underexposed, under pressure to perform, and under the thumb of a hard task master.

Have you ever said, "I'm under the weather," or "I'm underwater right now," or have you felt like you are under attack or under your circumstances? Well, you don't have to be under any of these anymore. According to Romans 16:20, the enemy has been put under your feet. Not only that, but you are also supposed to do something to the enemy. Do you know what it is? Crush that enemy! That is what the Good Book says. Yes, you can come out from under and learn to come out on top and be a triumphant overcomer.

Shame Off You!

Have you ever heard someone say, *"Shame on you!"* It's almost like they want to put slime on you and drag you down to their level so you cannot excel. Well, I have a word for you. "Shame off!" And I have a word for people saying things like that. "Stop it!"

Shame or guilt is like a bunch of crabs in a bucket. One usually starts to climb to the top to make its way out, but then the other crabs reach up and pull it back down to their level where they think it belongs, right in the smelly bottom of that bucket. Another crab gets the idea that it needs to breathe and tries to find some room of its own. It starts climbing its way towards the sky only to find the other crabs reaching up with their pinchers and pulling it down too.

I have seen this same practice happen way too often in Church culture, and God does not approve. It's time to quit playing these crab games inspired by the devil, and it's time for us to be cheerleaders in God's house instead of a bunch of crabs! The enemy is at the bottom of the bucket, so don't let him pull you down with him.

Living under the blame or accusation of the enemy, feeling guilt and shame, is oppressive and debilitating, causing mental, spiritual, and physical ailments. But let's look at the truth from Ephesians 2:4–6 that the devil does not want us to know:

> But God, being rich in mercy, because of His great love with which He loved us, even when we were dead in our wrongdoings, made us alive together with Christ (by grace you have been saved), and raised us up with Him, and seated us with Him in the heavenly places in Christ Jesus.

Where are we? In heavenly places in Christ Jesus. That means we are above and not beneath. We are over and not under. Ephesians 1:22 says, "He put all things in subjection under His [Jesus'] feet, and made Him head over all things." If we are seated with Christ in heavenly places, and all things are under His feet, then positionally everything is under our feet too.

So, if you've felt under the attack of the enemy, and if his accusations have buried you with guilt and shame, I declare to you, "Shame off you!" Too many of us live under shame, even for things that we did not do, but were done to us. The devil has no authority to put any guilt on you. If you feel guilt or shame hanging over your head, submit to the lordship of Jesus and shout, "Be quiet, accuser. I am forgiven and cleansed by the blood of Jesus. Shame off me in Jesus' name! Guilt off me in Jesus' name!"

The devil's business has changed because of John 12:31 (NLT), which says, "The time for judging this world has come, when Satan, the ruler of this world, will be cast out." Also, according to Colossians 2:15, God has now stripped Satan's principalities and powers of their weapons, the principle one being accusation. The Bible says that Jesus "shamed them publicly by his victory over them on the cross" (NLT). Did you get that? The enemy is the one who has shame, so don't let the devil put his shame on you.

As we conclude this section that has focused on the cross of Christ, remember that Jesus' death has defeated Satan and taken away his weapons and grounds of accusation. In short, the cross put Satan in his place: under our feet.

The apostle Paul concluded his letter to the Romans with these words: "The God of peace will soon crush Satan under your feet. May the grace of our Lord Jesus be with you" (16:20 NLT). The Passion Translation says, "And the God of peace will swiftly pound Satan to a pulp under your feet! And the wonderful favor of our Lord Jesus will surround you." I like that! Not only was the enemy's position changed by Christ's death, but we also anticipate Satan's complete destruction when Christ returns.

Let us be grounded in our place in Christ, firmly rooted in the foundation of His finished work on the cross, as we now turn to look at the weapons of our warfare.

FOR REFLECTION AND PRAYER

- How often are you struck by the enemy's weapons of accusation, shame, and guilt? How do you respond?
- What are common accusations the enemy uses against you? What is the truth according to the Word of God?
- How can you walk in the spiritual reality of being seated with Christ in heavenly places?

Talk to God about any blame, shame, or guilt you feel. Also be aware of the conviction of the Holy Spirit and confess any sins that come to mind. Then thank Jesus for your position in Him and ask Him to show you how to live in that reality each day.

VICTORIOUS SPIRITUAL WARFARE PRAYER

Father God, thank You for sending Your Son, Jesus, to destroy the works of the devil. I confess that I have fallen into sin, but I do not want to continue in darkness anymore. I choose to come into Your light and turn away from what does not honor You. Forgive me and cleanse me from all evil. Empower me by Your Spirit to walk in a manner that pleases You.

Heavenly Father, thank You that the completed work of the cross of Christ changed everything. Your Son, Jesus, bore my guilt and sin that I may have His righteousness. Jesus became a curse so I may receive the abundance of Your blessing. Jesus, my Messiah, experienced death so that I may receive life in this world and in the age to come. The divine exchange has taken place, and I am the recipient of Your great grace.

I want to cooperate with You and destroy the works of the devil just like Jesus did through His life and ministry, His death on the cross, and His powerful resurrection from the dead. I am alive with Christ and have been saved by His grace. You have seated me with Christ in heavenly places, and I live my life with You from that place. Hallelujah! Amen!

SECTION 6

YOUR WARFARE WEAPONS

In conclusion, be strong in the Lord [draw your strength from Him and be empowered through your union with Him] and in the power of His [boundless] might. Put on the full armor of God [for His precepts are like the splendid armor of a heavily-armed soldier], so that you may be able to [successfully] stand up against all the schemes and the strategies and the deceits of the devil. For our struggle is not against flesh and blood [contending only with physical opponents], but against the rulers, against the powers, against the world forces of this [present] darkness, against the spiritual forces of wickedness in the heavenly (supernatural) places. Therefore, put on the complete armor of God, so that you will be able to [successfully] resist and stand your ground in the evil day [of danger], and having done everything [that the crisis demands], to stand firm [in your place, fully prepared, immovable, victorious].

Ephesians 6:10–13 AMP

The next three chapters on the life-saving weapons of our warfare are vital, whether they are a review or are brand-new to you. A fresh look at the full armor of God will prepare you for your personal victory.

Do you want to be defeated by the devil, or would you like to defeat the devil yourself? I have had both happen in my life—and I much prefer defeating the devil and his cohorts.

I am not presenting the principles in this book to you as someone who has been victorious in every round of the "boxing match." The most appropriate way to describe the struggle Paul described is to imagine a boxing or wrestling match. Both are good analogies because these bouts consist of more than one round, and they represent a contact sport. Thank God we have more than one round in life.

Like me, you may get weak in one round and want to go back to your seat and take a break. You might say, "Been there, done that, and it's someone else's turn!" I get it. But guess what? There is a time to push pause, and there is a time to count the cost. There is a time to reevaluate, and there is a time to get reequipped and refreshed. And there is a time to reach into the Word and pull out the full armor of God, know that He is in your corner, and then reenter the arena.

Always remember, "Greater is He who is in you than he who is in the world" (1 John 4:4). You are not alone. If you're born again, a Warrior lives inside you—and He's the winner over all evil, disease, and suffering. Jesus overcame every battle, and He's the resurrected triumphant One. Jesus is the greatest weapon of spiritual warfare!

There are external weapons, and we're going to look at each of them. But the *greatest* weapon is the Man Christ Jesus who lives within you. Just as the well-known, traditional church hymn chorus declares:

"He lives! He lives! Christ Jesus lives today! He walks with me and talks with me along life's narrow way. He lives! He lives! Salvation to impart! You ask me how I know He lives? He lives within my heart."[1]

Usually sung during Easter services, this song helps us build the bridge between the spiritual and the physical, confirming that the greatest weapon of spiritual warfare is Christ Jesus who lives in your heart!

13

HOW WE CAN BE STRONG

A FRESH LOOK AT EPHESIANS 6:10-14

The world is enthralled with superheroes. Blockbuster movies are filled with heroes from the Fantastic Four, the Avengers, Superman, Wonder Woman, and the leading men and women in the latest versions of *Mission Impossible* and *Raiders of the Lost Ark*. We love a loser who becomes a winner, and we love it when supernatural strength enters the picture. Everything changes. We cheer when someone is just about to quit and then finally, just at the last minute, the atmosphere changes and a shift happens!

Ephesians 6:10–14 gives us Spirit-led insight for how we can remain strong until we see our triumph come into being. This passage starts out with the word *finally*. "Finally, be strong in the Lord and in the strength of His might." After all is said and done, after all the doctrine, the exhortations, and encouragements—there is one more thing. It's as if Paul is saying, "I saved the best for last. Now pay close attention. You are going to need this warfare strategy."

Some suggest that "finally" means "from now on," or "for the remaining time," and other Bible teachers refer to this as a period between the first and the second coming of Jesus. The idea is that from now on—at all times until Jesus comes again—we are at war. That's what Paul is saying. So be on the alert. Be ready. Be armed. Mostly likely the imagery of armor came to Paul from his observations of the Roman soldier to whom he was chained (see Ephesians 6:20). So let's look at the revelation God gave Paul about our warfare weapons.

Be Strong in the Lord (verse 10)

Paul did not say, "Finally, be strong. Come on! You can do this!" Self-reliance in spiritual warfare is both dangerous and useless. We are not called to war in our own strength. We are admonished to be strong *in the Lord*. Do you need that reminder? I know I do.

Other Scripture shows the strength of God's encouragement because He is with us. Joshua 1:6–9 records God's words to Joshua as he was about assume the leadership role Moses had occupied before his death. Three times the Lords tells Joshua to be strong and courageous, and at the end of verse 9 we see that Joshua's strength and courage is to be grounded in the reassuring promise that "the LORD your God is with you wherever you go."

And how about 1 Samuel 30:6 (NLT) as an example of God's unfailing presence? "David was now in great danger because all his men were very bitter about losing their sons and daughters, and they began to talk of stoning him." What happened next? David was greatly distressed, so he strengthened himself by scrolling through social media or watching Netflix? No! "David found strength in the LORD his God."

Second Chronicles 20:15 (NLT) records a prophetic word from God that Jehoshaphat received: "Listen, all you people of Judah and Jerusalem! Listen, King Jehoshaphat! This is what the LORD says: Do not be afraid! Don't be discouraged by this mighty army, for the battle is not yours, but God's." This is encouragement for you to give your battles to God. God will accept your battles and fight them for you—but you must give them to Him. God wants you to learn dependency on Him, to know that He is your sufficiency in all things, including emergencies.

I love the words of David recorded in Psalm 18:1, which says, "I love You, LORD, my strength." And Psalm 18:31–32 tells us, "For who is God, but the LORD? And who is our rock, except our God, the God who encircles me with strength, and makes my way blameless?" I love that! God encircles me with strength. So be it, Lord!

Another psalm of David records his heart when Saul sent soldiers to watch David's house to kill him. Psalm 59:16–17 says, "But as for me, I will sing of your strength. Yes, I will joyfully sing of Your faithfulness in the morning, for You have been my refuge and a place of refuge on the day of my distress. My strength, I will sing praises to You; for God is my refuge, the God who shows me favor." Wow!

We find the promise of God's strength again in Psalm 68:35: "The God of Israel Himself gives strength and power to the people. Blessed be God!" And Psalm 118:14 declares, "The LORD is my strength and song."

God wants to give us His strength when we need it. How do we access God's strength and power? Through prayer, fasting, by storing up the Word of God in our minds and our hearts, through fellowship and encouragement with others, through worship and praise, by taking the Lord's Supper, through the anointing and being filled with the Holy Spirit, and by putting on the full armor of God. There are many ways to receive the strength of God.

Put On the Full Armor of God (Verse 11)

You were not born wearing God's armor. You must take the time and make the effort to put on each piece, and once you have the full armor on, leave it on. Walk in it, work in it, and sleep in it.

Do everything while wearing your armor. Many Christians put it on and take it off depending on their circumstances. To be always protected, you must always wear the full armor of God at all times.

After Paul says to "be strong in the Lord and in the strength of His might," he instructs, "Put on the full armor of God, so that you will be able to stand firm against the schemes of the devil."

Two prominent Old Testament texts couple armor and God's traits. Isaiah 11:4 says, "Righteousness will be the belt around His hips, and faithfulness the belt around His waist." And Isaiah 59:17 says, "He put on righteousness as a breastplate, and a helmet of salvation on His head; and He put on garments of vengeance for clothing and wrapped Himself with zeal as a cloak."

While we will look at specific parts of our spiritual armor in future chapters, I want to declare loudly that God Himself is our Warrior. Your most effective spiritual warfare weapon is God Himself. If you are born again, Jesus lives inside you—Christ in you, the hope of glory (see Colossians 1:27).

God the Warrior is fighting to deliver and vindicate His children. The supernatural armor, which God Himself wears, has been graciously made available to us. In other words, it is the armor of God not simply because He gives it, but because He wears it. It is heaven's armament released onto the earth so that we can stand firm against the schemes of the devil.

What are the schemes of the devil? Evil tactics, secret agendas, temptations, accusations, intimidation, division, and other such assaults against individual believers—including systematic, institutional, and organizational stratagems and strategic plans against not just the Church, but societies worldwide.

While we can look at Scripture and history and see common schemes of the devil, I do not believe all his methods and tactics are explicitly revealed in Scripture. This is all the more reason to wear the *full* armor, not just part of it. Last days battles require the body of Christ to be fully armed!

Our Struggle (Verse 12)

Ephesians 6:10 tells us to be strong in the Lord, not our own strength. Verse 11 makes us aware of God's complete armor that helps us to stand against the enemy's schemes. Then verse 12 shows us the nature of our battle against the enemy: it's a spiritual struggle.

The Greek term translated for "struggle" is *pale* (*Strong's* #3823) meaning "wrestling." This "wrestling match" expression is used only once in the New Testament. Why did Paul use this sporting term pertaining to armor and military preparedness? Why not use the same words as found in 2 Corinthians 10:4 or 1 Timothy 1:8—*strategia* or *strateia* (*Strong's* #4752)—which mean "warfare"? The reason is very significant.

Wrestling was an extremely popular event in athletic games held in Asia Minor, particularly in Ephesus, where Paul preached for a few years. In contrast to the flesh and blood wrestling that the readers in Ephesus would have been very familiar with, the true struggle of believers is a spiritual power encounter that requires spiritual weaponry.

New Testament scholar Clinton Arnold explains the following beliefs Ephesians had in the magical arts during the time of Paul:

> Two ancient writers relate the humorous account of an Ephesian wrestler who traveled to Olympia, Greece, to compete in the Olympic games. The wrestler attached an amulet to his ankle that had the Ephesian letters inscribed on it. These were six magical names, probably referring to six powerful supernatural beings. The Ephesian wrestler was readily defeating his opponents and advancing in the event until the referee discovered the ankle bracelet! He then lost three successive matches.[1]

Clinton Arnold believes that Paul may have been alluding to this story with this use of the word *pale*. He continues:

> The allusion could have proved an effective way of communicating to the converts that they should no longer "put on" the Ephesia

Grammata as an amulet (i.e. turn to magic), but should now "put on" the armor of God (i.e. the power of God). Furthermore, they would also understand in a fresh way that the struggle in which they have been enlisted as Christians is against supernatural "powers"—in fact, the very supernatural "powers" who were summoned to their aid by the Ephesia Grammata are now the attacking opponents which they need to resist![2]

Wrestling is a close encounter contact game in which you must pin your enemy, not once, but many times. It is in-your-face and hand-to-hand combat. Knowing the historical context reveals even more about the struggle with our own spiritual enemy.

This struggle is "not against flesh and blood." Paul is saying that our struggle is not against humanity. Behind and beneath the daily earthly struggles with people, institutions, and ideologies is an unseen spiritual battle. We may have earthly and human antagonists, but we must realize that Satan works behind their efforts (also see Matthew 16:23).

Standing Firm (Verses 11, 13, and 14)

Three times Paul tells the Ephesians to stand firm in verses 11, 13, and 14. He didn't just say to stand. He said to stand *firm*. This means we are to hold our position, resist, refuse to surrender ground to the enemy, preserve, and maintain what has already been won.

How are we supposed to stand firm? With the full armor of God. The New Living Translation says we resist the enemy with "every piece of God's armor." Before Paul introduces the individual pieces of God's armor, he says we need all of it. Why? "So that you will be able to resist on the evil day, and having done everything, to stand firm" (verse 13).

The "evil day" could be describing the entire present age, or occasions when the attack is especially intense, or possibly both.

Regardless, with God's full armor, we can stand firm in whatever season we find ourselves.

What you need to fight in one season is not the same as the next. After Jesus' forty-day fast, the Bible says, "And he [the devil] departed from him [Jesus] for a season" (Luke 4:13 KJV). The devil didn't leave Him permanently. The New Living Translation states, "When the devil had finished tempting Jesus, he left him until the next opportunity came."

Harassment can come from the enemy at times of the greatest potential in God. That is when God wants you to seek Him and find Him and push through that door into new opportunities.

FOR REFLECTION AND PRAYER

- How often do you find yourself leaning on your own strength instead of finding your strength in the Lord?
- What has been your experience with the "full armor of God," and how have you used it in everyday life?
- What happens when you start to battle with people instead of the enemy behind the struggle? How interconnected are these two realms in your day-to-day reality and how can you position yourself to fight the true enemy?

Ask God to show you afresh the strength He has for you as you wrestle and the complete armor He's provided for your triumph.

14

Spiritual Weapons with Divine Power

A FRESH LOOK AT 2 CORINTHIANS 10:3-5

Let's look at another letter Paul sent to the early Church that talks about weapons of warfare. Paul wrote:

> For though we live in the world, we do not wage war as the world does. The weapons we fight with are not the weapons of the world. On the contrary, they have divine power to demolish strongholds. We demolish arguments and every pretension that sets itself up against the knowledge of God, and we take captive every thought to make it obedient to Christ.
>
> 2 Corinthians 10:3–5 NIV

Paul made it very clear that even though we are humans who live in the world, we do not use the human weapons the world uses. In other words, we live and minister in flesh-and-blood bodies, but we do not utilize its tactics and schemes to achieve our goals.

Have you ever considered that you have weapons that have *divine* powers? So many movies now exist about superheroes and superpowers. You may not be able to fly, make yourself small, or be invisible, but you have divine powers! God has given you spiritual weapons that are divinely powerful. Declare with me right now, "My spiritual weapons are divinely powerful for the destruction of strongholds and fortresses in Jesus' name!"

Our weapons are divinely effective and get the job done because God works in and through them. They're made powerful by God, and they are powerful for God.

The Weapons God Provides

Since our adversaries are spiritual, our weapons must also be spiritual. In the next section we'll look at six specific pieces we commonly call the armor of God. But did you know our spiritual weapons extend beyond that list? Yes, God gives us truth, righteousness, peace, faith, salvation, and the Word of God. He also gives us the Holy Spirit (remember that God Himself is our greatest weapon), perseverance, assurance, alertness, prayer, praise, boldness and more.

Human ingenuity, beauty and eloquence, excellence and grand effort, soulish wisdom, showmanship, the power of persuasion and command in public speaking, and sparkle and charm might take you places and even promote you before man. But these traits coupled with a persuasive personality devoid of the Spirit will eventually result in a crash.

What is the goal of our weapons anyway? To persuade or make a show for personal gain? Absolutely not. The purpose of our weapons is to destroy the works of the enemy in every area of life. We use our weapons to "demolish arguments and every pretension that sets itself up against the knowledge of God, and we take captive every thought to make it obedient to Christ" (2 Corinthians 10:5).

Arguments, speculations, thoughts, and intentions are spiritual in nature, which is why we must use spiritual weapons to demolish them. Our weapons can destroy (adjust) the way other people think and demolish sinful thought patterns and mental structures by which they live their lives in rebellion against God. In other words, every arrogant claim, every haughty or prideful thought, and every selfish act form a barrier to the knowledge of God. These arguments rationalize sin, promote unbelief, and delay repentance.

The Message interprets 2 Corinthians 10:5 this way:

> The world is unprincipled. It's dog-eat-dog out there! The world doesn't fight fair. But we don't live or fight our battles that way— never have and never will. The tools of our trade aren't for marketing or manipulation, but they are for demolishing that entire massively corrupt culture. We use our powerful God-tools for smashing warped philosophies, tearing down barriers erected against the truth of God, fitting every loose thought and emotion and impulse into the structure of life shaped by Christ. Our tools are ready at hand for clearing the ground of every obstruction and building lives of obedience into maturity.

God has given us divine, spiritual weapons to fight our battles. They are so powerful they dismantle and tear down sinful reasoning and rationalizations, which left unchecked influence the mind against the Gospel. We are called to "take every thought captive to the obedience of Christ." When we do that, we come into a new allegiance and alliance with the Kingdom of God and advance the plan of God for His world.

I love every time I see my friend Michael W. Smith throw back his head and sing with all his heart the song "Surrounded (Fight My Battles)." "This is how I fight my battles!" Yes, when things aren't looking good, God surrounds us and fights our battles for us and with us! *Thank You, Jesus, for Your spiritual weapons that are divinely powerful for the tearing down of demonic strongholds.*

132

—— FOR REFLECTION AND PRAYER ——

- Your weapons have divine power—not human, worldly, or fleshly power. Each time each one is divinely effective. Do you believe that truth? Do you realize how heavily armed you are? That your victory is assured?

- How have you seen spiritual weapons address spiritual problems in your life such as sinful arguments or rationalizations?

- When you fire a physical weapon such as a pistol or rifle, there is significant recoil or kickback that can stun the shooter. Thinking about your spiritual weapons, what type of kickback have you seen or should you expect?

Take a few moments right now to talk to God about spiritual issues around you that require His spiritual weapons. Ask Him for discernment about which weapons the Holy Spirit wants you to use in each situation.

15

THE POWER BEHIND THE ARMOR

Let's read 2 Corinthians 10:3–4 (NLT) once again:

> We are human, but we don't wage war as humans do. We use God's mighty weapons, not worldly weapons, to knock down the strongholds of human reasoning and to destroy false arguments.

Some have misinterpreted and thus misapplied this passage and the following verse as if it was only speaking of cosmic-level spiritual warfare—in other words, territorial spirits or spirits that influence geographical areas, which we will look at in another chapter. Primarily, "strongholds," "arguments and every high thing" (verse 5 NKJV) have been taken as a reference to demonic spirits only. But the enemies Paul is referring to in this passage are ideas, arguments, philosophies, and excuses that are antithetical to the Kingdom of God and the glory of God.

What does Paul say to do? "We demolish arguments and every pretension that sets itself up against the knowledge of God, and we take captive every thought to make it obedient to Christ" (verse

5 NIV). Who is behind these thoughts, structures, stratagems, and these structural ways of thinking?

We can look at Scripture that says before we were born again, we were controlled by "the prince of the power of the air . . . and lusts of our flesh" (Ephesians 2:1–3), and that our minds had been "darkened in their understanding" (Ephesians 4:17–19) and "blinded" by the god of this world so that we did not "see the light of the gospel of the glory of Christ" (2 Corinthians 4:4).

Regardless of who is behind them, God wants us to see what—and Who—is behind our armor and how we demolish the works of the enemy.

The Holy Spirit and the Word

Years ago, I was in Sarajevo, the capital and largest city of Bosnia–Herzegovina, ministering with Mahesh Chavda, a dear mentor friend. After Mahesh had prayed for people, we noticed a man lying on his back on the floor. The man, who did not speak English, was curled up in a ball. He was in agony and his extremities were turning cold and blue, so Mahesh asked me to follow up in prayer for this man.

Through an interpreter I tried to understand what was going on. I could not. Even my experience and gift to discern spirits did not help me in this situation to determine what this man needed. I called out to the Holy Spirit and understood that this man was up against a stronghold. I addressed the power of darkness out loud with a gift of faith and asked, "What is the hindrance?" This man who could not speak English miraculously said, "Take the book out."

We turned the man over and discovered he had a book in his hip pocket—*Mein Kampf*, a political manifesto written by Adolf Hitler. When we pulled that book out of his pocket, the man was instantly set free of all demonic harassment. He accepted the Lord Jesus Christ as his Savior and was filled with the Holy Spirit. We learned through the interpreter that the man was from Hungary, attending the University of Sarajevo, studying philosophy and communism. The demonic stronghold that bound this man was the book that espoused an evil philosophy.

How was this stronghold exposed? The Holy Spirit brought it to light as I listened to His words. It was not until I asked the Holy Spirit for help that I learned what was going on. Even though I was wearing the armor of God and had been operating in the gifts of the Spirit for years, it was the present-tense voice of the Spirit that became my warfare weapon to expose the stronghold so I could deal with it under the anointing.

We need all our spiritual weapons to deal with these strongholds—especially the stealthy ones. Who would have guessed that a book in a man's back pocket would be a key to setting him free? And who would have thought that man would supernaturally be given the gift of English to speak the answer?

Christians can also have strongholds. Intellectual, philosophical, and moral enemies of the Kingdom of God don't automatically disappear when we get saved. God does not give us a scrub brush, cleanse our brain, and then we automatically have a new mind. I wish it were so. It is up to us to "be transformed by the renewing of your mind" (Romans 12:2).

In chapter 9 I shared Ed Silvoso's definition of a stronghold: "a mindset impregnated with hopelessness that forces you to accept as unchangeable, situations or outcomes that you know are contrary to the will of God."[1] Strongholds can be negative patterns of thought that cripple our ability to obey God, which can bring guilt and despair that get burned into our minds, either through repetition over time or through a traumatic experience.

So how can you destroy strongholds? Fill your mind with God's Word. "Fix your thoughts on what is true, and honorable, and right, and pure, and lovely, and admirable. Think about things that are excellent and worthy of praise" (Philippians 4:8 NLT). Challenge every negative, destructive thought the instant it enters your mind. Learn to turn off the receiver of any thoughts that are contrary to the Word of God.[2] The Word of God and the present-tense voice of the Holy Spirit are the power behind your armor.

Warfare Prayer

English poet and hymn writer William Cowper wrote: "Restraining pray'r, we cease to fight; pray'r makes the Christian's armor bright; and Satan trembles when he sees the weakest saint upon his knees."[3]

Except on rare occasions, God will not intervene to give you daily victory—unless you ask Him. There are different views on that statement. I personally believe that in God's sovereignty, He chose to give man the power of free choice to partner with Him. When we choose to partner with God, we invite Him through the power of prayer to extend the Kingdom of God on earth as it is in heaven. God has done it all, but He also invites us into the process of enforcing the victory of Calvary (more details about this coming later).

Prayer is not specifically mentioned as the seventh piece of our spiritual armor in Ephesians 6:18, nor is it the way we wield the sword of the Spirit, which is the Word of God. But grammatically Paul connects standing firm with praying and being alert. You can see the connection better if you remove the verses on the armor: "Stand firm [with every piece of armor and] . . . with every prayer and request, pray at all times in the Spirit, and with this in view, be alert with all perseverance" (Ephesians 6:14, 18).

Prayer is what characterizes and permeates the whole Christian soldier's activity. Prayer is how we stay alert in full armor. Take your stand as you pray. Put on the belt of truth praying. Put on the breastplate of righteousness as you pray. So is prayer the seventh piece of armor? I believe it could be. Is prayer the piece that holds it all together? Is prayer what is behind the armor? I definitely believe it is.

As triumphant believers in Christ and as sons or daughters of the Most High God, the King of glory, we are given divinely powerful spiritual weapons. Right now, choose to listen to the Holy Spirit, read the Word of God, and pray as we clothe ourselves in the full armor of God.

It is in this place that we are strengthened with the strength of the Lord. We choose to walk in the light where the blood of Jesus cleanses us from all sin, and we then go into a position of rest, where we are now fully clothed in the new nature in Christ Jesus our Lord!

FOR REFLECTION AND PRAYER

- What human reasoning and false arguments have you encountered that seek to undermine the Kingdom of God and the glory of God?
- How is the Word of God, the voice of the Holy Spirit, and prayer the power behind the armor and absolutely necessary in spiritual warfare?

Take a few moments to talk to God right now about any human reasoning or false arguments that have gotten in the way of your walk with Jesus.

VICTORIOUS SPIRITUAL WARFARE PRAYER

Heavenly God of War, I declare that my warfare is aimed at dismantling and tearing down ungodly reasoning, rationalizations, and strongholds by which my mind fortifies itself against the Gospel of Your Kingdom. I take those thoughts captive by Your grace and teach my mind to hear the Word of God and obey it. With the aid of the Holy Spirit, I will renew my mind in Your will, Your Word, and Your ways. I want to be a warrior in Your Kingdom, and so I listen to the voice of the Holy Spirit and I pray.

Help me see with fresh eyes the battle I am in, for even though I live in the world, I do not fight like the world does. I know by faith that my Holy Spirit–saturated prayers are effective spiritual weapons that hold everything together for Your glory. Thank You, Jesus, that You are my greatest Weapon in spiritual warfare. I look to You, and I fight with You, my Mighty Warrior. Amen and amen.

THE ARMOR OF GOD

Stand firm therefore, having belted your waist with truth, and having put on the breastplate of righteousness, and having strapped on your feet the preparation of the gospel of peace; in addition to all, taking up the shield of faith with which you will be able to extinguish all the flaming arrows of the evil one. And take the helmet of salvation and the sword of the Spirit, which is the word of God.

Ephesians 6:14–17

Anytime I think of the armor of God, I immediately remember the precious days when my children were young. They would create swords, shields, belts, and funny helmets out of whatever construction paper and tape—lots of tape—they could find. It was fun, tangible, and part of family life that brought the Bible alive.

I especially remember when I took my oldest son, Justin, on a trip with me to North Dakota when he was about seven years old. While I ministered, he played in a side room with sheets of long blue construction paper, lots of tape, and scissors. I prophetically told the people crazy dreams about cities that would be built and mineral finds and natural gas reserves just waiting to make their impoverished wastelands rich. I even drew out on a board how big and broad this economic impact would be for North Dakota and spill over into South Dakota. They sat there wondering if I was from Mars!

Then Justin emerged dressed up in a complete suit of the armor of God, proudly hoisting his shield of faith and ready to swing his sword of the Spirit that he had just made. He went into that side room a shy boy and came out commanding the attention of those who had gathered.

This simple act somehow seemed to shift the spiritual atmosphere because they took my words seriously. Years later, all of those words came to pass as North Dakota flourished with new fields of natural gas and wealth poured into that once impoverished state.

The armor of God is not just for children to act out for a fun Sunday school lesson or at vacation Bible school. Each weapon of God's armor is for every believer, every day, all the time. Without the armor of God, we are not "able to resist on the evil day, and having done everything, to stand firm" (Ephesians 6:13).

So let's look then at the armor God has provided that enables us to stand our ground against the enemy.

16

TRUTH AND RIGHTEOUSNESS

Imagine you just signed up to be in the military, knowing that you were headed straight into battle on the front lines of the war. You've heard the casualties are high, and even the best warriors are getting injured—or even worse, sacrificing their lives. You are standing in a line, vulnerable and empty handed, waiting to see what they will give you to take into battle.

In this moment when you are about to receive armor and instructions that will literally save your life, how attentive are you? Your life and the lives of others depend on what follows. I hope you're leaning in, eager to hear and remember every word. Remember, you were born in a war, and you were born for war! Let us, therefore, be attentive to the Word of God as He tells us about His weapons and how to use them.

The Belt of Truth (Ephesians 6:14)

Ephesians 6:14 says, "Stand firm therefore, having belted your waist with truth." The New King James translation says, "having girded your waist with truth." This was not simply a strip of cloth around the waist, or even a narrow belt to hold up one's pants. It was a leather apron that helped protect the lower part of the body. This "belt" had two additional functions. First, it was used to hold up the sheath for the soldier's sword, the offensive weapon of the warrior. Second, the soldier's tunic clothing would be tucked into or under this belt whenever fighting or running. What is this truth God invites us to strap around our waists?

Jesus is truth. Jesus said of Himself, "I am . . . the truth" (John 14:6). As Jesus stood before Pontius Pilate after He had been betrayed, He said, "For this purpose I have been born, and for this I have come into the world: to testify to the truth. Everyone who is of the truth listens to My voice" (John 18:37–39).

To put on the belt of truth is to testify that Jesus is the truth. And when we put on Christ (see Romans 13:14), we clothe ourselves with truth—with His character.

George Mallone writes, "In warfare, we must be surrounded by absolute truthfulness. The issue is not just doctrinal truth, but personal truthfulness. To stop the enemy, we must stop lying, whether by exaggeration or understatement, but put on integrity in all we do and say."[1] Winning in the area of spiritual warfare is first and foremost an issue and question of character as we align with the truth of Jesus.

The Bible is truth. Second Timothy 2:15 says, "Be diligent to present yourself approved to God as a worker who does not need to be ashamed, accurately handling the word of truth." Successful spiritual warfare begins with these questions: *Do I accept the Bible as God's Word inspired, infallible, and the sole authority for belief and practice? Do I have the truth of God living in me? Do I believe the truth?*

The Church is the pillar of truth. First Timothy 3:14–15 tells us, "I am writing these things to you, hoping to come to you before long; but in case I am delayed, I write so that you will know how one should act in the household of God, which is the church of the living God, the pillar and support of the truth." The Church is often referred to as the *Ekklesia*, the called-out ones of God. We assemble as disciples of Christ Jesus walking under the banner of His Lordship and submit to His delegated godly leadership— providing protection, reinforcement of biblical virtues, encouragement, stability, and guidance. I know that the Church has its faults; but friend, we are still called to assemble and encourage each other regularly (see Hebrews 3:13; 10:25).

The truth of Christian doctrine. Satan will always flourish where there is theological ignorance. My oh my, is that ever the truth today! There are two areas in which demonic lies are most prevalent and powerful. One, lies about God—His character and attributes. And two—and this is why we have to wear truth—lies about yourself, who you are, your identity and position in Christ, and your authority and power.

The truth may also refer to "truthfulness," the integrity of speech and behavior. Truthfulness is the absence of duplicity or hypocrisy. The time in which we live is full of duplicity and entitlement, but we must all put on truth and refuse to take part in lying or deception. And remember, we need to take the log out of our own eye before we can point at others.

The Breastplate of Righteousness (Ephesians 6:14)

"Put on the breastplate of righteousness" (Ephesians 6:14). The word in the Greek for *breastplate* is *thorax* (*Strong's* #2382). This piece of armor usually extends from the base of the neck to the upper part of the thighs, covering what we would call the abdomen or the trunk of our body. Essential organs that must be functional to live, such as the heart and lungs, are protected by the breastplate. This piece of armor is essential to life!

George Mallone writes the following:

> It is true that any righteousness we have is given to us by God, through faith (Rom 5:1). But righteousness, in the context of Ephesians 6,

refers to character and conduct. Jesus was convinced the devil had nothing on him (Jn 14:30). There was no sin to exploit, no accusations to lodge. Likewise, personal righteousness, holiness and integrity, forbids the devil from having anything on us. It is our protection from exploitation.[2]

The Bible compares our righteous deeds to a filthy garment (see Isaiah 64:6). Any righteousness we have is a gift from God "through faith in Jesus Christ for all those who believe" (Romans 3:22). Have you received this priceless gift?

You may have noticed that today we don't like the word *righteousness*. But it's in the Bible and without it we cannot see God or live for Him (see Matthew 5:8; Galatians 3:11). In fact, it's important to see that all the pieces of the armor are connected so we can be victorious in battle.

Righteousness is interconnected with faith and love. Paul instructed the Church to "be sober, putting on faith and love as a breastplate" (1 Thessalonians 5:8 NIV). Derek Prince adds to this:

> That is the breastplate that we need, one that never fails, a breastplate in which there are no weak points that Satan can penetrate. And see how appropriate what Paul says there is to the picture of the breastplate. Love always protects, always trusts, always hopes, always perseveres. When you have on that breastplate of faith that works by love, it will always protect you.[3]

Remember, the breastplate covers the essential organs. "It will keep your heart from every attack and attempt of Satan to penetrate that vital area of your life."[4]

Positional and Outworked Righteousness

I mentioned above that God considers our own righteous deeds a filthy garment, yet we have been "created in Christ Jesus for good works, which God prepared beforehand so that we would walk in them" (Ephesians 2:10). So my works are filthy, but I've been created for good works? Which is it?

To explain this seeming contradiction, let's consider if this "breastplate of righteousness" is positional, objective, and imputed. Or is it outworked, subjective, and imparted? Or possibly both?

- *Positional righteousness or truth* is the gift of God we receive when we trust in Jesus and His sacrifice for us on the cross. You do not earn it and you do not deserve it. It is a gift by grace, and in that sense could be called "positional truth" because God positions us in Jesus who is the truth. This righteousness is yours as a free gift in Christ Jesus (see Romans 4:4–5; 2 Corinthians 5:21; Philippians 3:8–9).
- *Outworked righteousness or truthfulness* is doing what is right, living according to God's standards, and pursuing what is right in our daily lives (see 1 Timothy 6:11; Ephesians 4:24; 5:9). For more on this subject, see my book *A Radical Faith: Essentials for Spirit-Filled Believers* regarding these two biblical truths.
- *Objective* righteousness is our position of standing through faith in Christ and Christ alone. Some might refer to this as the breastplate of our justification, which is our legally bought and sealed grace gift of holiness (see Philippians 3; 2 Corinthians 5:21; Romans 3:19–24).
- *Subjective* righteousness is the breastplate of experiential holiness of life—experiencing it and walking it out or owning it for ourselves (see Ephesians 4:24; 5:9).

Not knowing the difference between positional objective and outworked subjective righteousness trips up a lot of people. We must realize we need both: We are already seated with Christ in the heavenly places, wearing robes of pure white linen of the gift of righteousness, *and* we must pursue righteousness in our daily lives by walking in the cleansing fires of sanctification, purity, and holiness by the power of the Holy Spirit.

James 2:20 helps us understand the need for both. This pragmatic apostolic teacher understood that "faith without works is dead." You could also flip it around to say it this way, "Faith without corresponding actions is a dead corpse."

As we combine these thoughts, we gather a combined truth: Faith with corresponding actions is life from the dead. In the same way we need faith and actions, we also need to receive the righteousness of Christ and choose righteousness daily.

—— FOR REFLECTION AND PRAYER ——

- Consider if you believe there is absolute truth from God, the Bible, and the Church that can be known. Or are people simply accountable to their own truth? How protective is a belt that consists of truth of your own making versus truth that is clear from the Word of God?
- What difference do you see between positional righteousness and outworked righteousness? On which side do you most naturally lean? How can you fully embrace both equally?

Take a few moments right now to talk to God about the truth He has revealed to you. Are you all in? Then thank Him for His positional righteousness and ask the Holy Spirit to help you work out areas of holy living He wants to address in your life.

17

PUTTING ON THE ARMOR PIECE BY PIECE

Remember that the apostle Paul emphasized that we must put on the *full* armor of God, piece by piece. With that in mind, let's look at the remaining four pieces of the armor God gives to use in spiritual warfare: the shoes of peace, shield of faith, helmet of salvation, and sword of the Spirit.

Shoes of Peace

Ephesians 6:15 instructs us to strap on our feet "the preparation of the gospel of peace." When I think about the shoes of God's armor, my dear friend Cindy Jacobs comes to mind because she wears red shoes as a signature part of her wardrobe. In fact, the warrior women in Cindy's "Global Deborah Company" wear red shoes, which represent the blood of Jesus, raising up conservative moral believers and inspiring women to make a positive difference in their churches, homes, marketplace, and communities, and in every sphere of influence in the world.

We must put the right thing on our feet! Our shoes are vitally important to our health, our capacity to stand, and even the way we appear. And of course, there are different types of shoes for different types of engagements. You don't wear football cleats to a ballroom dance! Always remember, though, that the Bride of Christ does wear army boots!

The shoes of the Roman legionaries, however, were not red shoes with heels. They were usually strong, heavy sandals with interlacing thongs to keep them in place. They were usually laced at least halfway up the calf with leather straps. These shoes were a vital part of the legionary's equipment, enabling him to march long distances at a quick pace, giving him mobility and freedom of movement. His shoes made him available to his commander at the time and the place where he was needed in the battle. Think of your shoes as providing mobility and availability to your Commander, the Lord Jesus Christ. What a responsibility and privilege!

Having prepared feet sounds somewhat like Isaiah 52:7 (NIV) and the activity of evangelism: "How beautiful on the mountains are the feet of those who bring good news." The King James Version of Ephesians 6:15 says, "And your feet shod with the preparation of the gospel of peace." *Shod* means shoed, covered, and dressed; therefore, our feet are prepared or ready to proclaim the glorious gospel of peace.

The New International Version of the Bible translates Ephesians 6:15 this way: "With your feet fitted with the readiness that comes from the gospel of peace." The term *fitted* most likely means the shoes were a good fit and would not come off easily. When our shoes fit perfectly, we can move throughout our day confidently and at a good pace.

The Gospel is the power of God by which people are set free from Satan's captivity and tyranny. Because our feet are fitted "with the readiness that comes from the gospel of peace," the Gospel produces in us the *readiness* to obey Jesus' call to go and share the Gospel with others. This piece of the armor does not produce the urgency to preach the Gospel, but it does help us to get going! At this point and time, we need to line up and be like track stars. Ready, set, go!

Also notice that the Gospel is the "gospel of peace." Many people who rush out to share the Gospel are not filled with peace. The peace that the Gospel produces in us is to prepare us for Satan's attacks as we go—peace *with* God and the peace *of* God. And how about peace with others (see Romans 12:18). The "gospel of peace," therefore, refers either to the peace *in* the Gospel, which we proclaim, or to the peace *of* the Gospel, which we experience within ourselves and with others.

I believe it is both because we encounter *and* experience the Gospel. Let's not become overfamiliar with what we think the Gospel is that we miss the important element of peace. The peace of God is a central part in the Kingdom of God found only in the Holy Spirit (see Romans 14:17).

Taking Up Your Shield of Faith

Ephesians 6:16 says, "in addition to all, taking up the shield of faith with which you will be able to extinguish all the flaming arrows of the evil one." There are two types of shields represented in the New Testament. One is a small, circular shield, shaped more like a large, round wicker basket. The other one is a long, rectangular shield, taken from the word *door* because of its shape. This is the kind of shield Paul speaks of when he says to take up the shield of faith—not the small circular one, the large one shaped like a door.

This shield was probably about two feet wide and four feet long. It was made of two layers of wood glued together and covered first with linen and then with an animal hide. It was bound on the top and bottom with iron. Its purpose was to defend against the incendiary missiles of the enemy—arrows dipped in pitch, set aflame, and launched.

For further protection, the shield was soaked in water to extinguish any flame on contact. The shield not only protected the individual soldiers, but also many soldiers when they stood together with their shields side by side and then moved forward toward the enemy. Like a modern tank, these warriors banded together posed a great military threat.

The flaming arrows of the evil one

The flaming arrows mentioned in Ephesians 6:16 come as sudden and unexpected interruptions of vile images and thoughts in our minds, which surprise us and are obviously and undeniably contrary to our basic desires as followers of Jesus. These arrows are words and pictures that violate your God-given sense of morality. Some examples of these flaming arrows can include blasphemous thoughts, revolting images, suicidal urges, compulsive thoughts, uncountable impulses, subtle insinuations, and false feelings of guilt.

The enemy commonly flings these arrows at us as we are reading the Bible, praying, or praising God—not when reading worldly magazines or newspapers. This can produce feelings of personal guilt and worthlessness. We think, *What kind of a person am I that I would have such thoughts and fantasies precisely when I'm trying to love God and worship Him?* The enemy's fiery arrows assault us so we stop doing what is the most important—spending time with God.

Time spent with God is vital to our spiritual well-being. The evil one knows that, and that is why he chooses then to attack us. At such times when we are reading His Word, praying, and worshiping Him, we are actually walking through a mental minefield. Always remember that greater is God who lives in you than the evil in the world (see 1 John 4:4).

Keep concentrating on Jesus, and you will be strengthened to hold up that shield of faith, and those fiery darts of the enemy will be extinguished. Yes, they will!

What is this faith Paul describes?

There are three kinds of faith in the Christian life:

1. *Saving faith*—the product of the new birth. Every person, according to Romans 12:3, has a measure of faith.
2. *Sanctifying faith*—a fruit of the Holy Spirit's work in our lives—outworked righteousness as listed in Galatians 5:22, often called faithfulness.
3. *Supernatural faith*—the spontaneous gift of the Holy Spirit mentioned in various places in the Word of God (see 1 Corinthians 12:9).

What is faith? Faith is not so much a quality we possess, but a relationship to which we have access. Any movement toward God comprises two actions. First, we must believe that God is. We affirm His nature as a verb, not an adjective. Hebrews 11:6 says: "And without faith it is impossible to please Him, for the one who comes to God must believe that He exists, and that He proves to be One who rewards those who seek Him." Second, we must believe that God rewards those who seek Him. We must fight to trust in God's promise to reward us for seeking Him, pressing away doubt, and resisting the ways of self-reliance. Our efforts are truly noted in heaven. He is the Rewarder!

There is a whole lot more on faith that I encourage you to study on your own. Remember that your shield is no ordinary shield. It is a shield of faith! When Satan whispers, "God doesn't care about you," lift your shield of faith and say, "That's impossible. God so loved the world that He gave His Son for me. Nothing in all creation can ever separate me from the love of God."

The Helmet of Salvation

Ephesians 6:17 says, "And take the helmet of salvation and the sword of the Spirit, which is the word of God." Since the principal battleground in spiritual warfare is the mind, we have the need for the helmet of protection, a spiritual hard hat, if you will. The Roman helmet was made of tough metal, either bronze or iron, with a hinged visor for protection. This image also appears in Isaiah 59:17 (NLT) as the Messiah, wearing His own helmet of salvation, comes to deliver those who have repented: "He put on righteousness as his body armor and placed the helmet of salvation on his head. He clothed himself with a robe of vengeance and wrapped himself in a cloak of divine passion."

How do we use the helmet of salvation to protect our minds? First, we must affirm that we already have the mind of Christ by the Holy Spirit: "For, 'Who can know the Lord's thoughts? Who knows enough to teach him?' But we understand these things, for we have the mind of Christ" (1 Corinthians 2:16 NLT).

Second, we ask Jesus to help us place before Him all our major thoughts, feelings, and motives that have been a part of our day. Then ask Him, "What is Your perspective on these thoughts, feelings, and motives? Give me Your mind." We can have the mind of Christ on these matters, and when we have received it, we then must graft God's thoughts into our minds.

James 1:21 (NLT) shows us how this happens: "So get rid of all the filth and evil in your lives, and humbly accept the word God has planted in your hearts, for it has the power to save your souls." James is not speaking of first-time new-birth salvation when we receive Jesus as Lord and Savior. James is saying that every part of the soul—mind, will, and emotions—is affected when we get rid of evil and receive God's Word into our hearts.

We plant God's thoughts into our hearts and minds by studying, reading, meditating, and memorizing Scripture in the areas where we need help. We allow our minds to become renewed and refreshed. Romans 12:2 (NLT) tells us clearly:

> Don't copy the behavior and customs of this world, but let God transform you into a new person by changing the way you think.

Then you will learn to know God's will for you, which is good and pleasing and perfect.

According to 1 Thessalonians 5:8, the helmet is the *hope* of salvation. Hope is the vital, positive expectation of good—and God has Good News for you! First Thessalonians 5:9–11 (emphasis added) boldly declares,

> God has not destined us for wrath, but for *obtaining salvation through our Lord Jesus Christ,* who died for us, so that whether we are awake or asleep, we will live together with Him. Therefore, encourage one another and build one another up, just as you also are doing.

Hope is an optimistic attitude that always chooses to see the best and will not give way to negativity. I have to work on this one. How about you? Hope does not give way to depression, doubt, and self-pity. The mystery of all this is profoundly summed up in Colossians 1:27, "Christ in you, the hope of glory." If Christ is in you, you have hope. Period.

In the middle of battle, don't lose your hope. A person in battle can lose a finger, an arm, or even two legs. But if you lose your head, you're dead! In the words of Hebrews 6:18–19, "Hold firmly to the hope set before us. This hope we have as an anchor of the soul." When we keep our minds fixed on the God of hope, our helmet stays firmly on our heads as we fight our battles. In fact, I have written an entire transparent narrative about my personal journey of discovering hope called *Tell Your Heart to Sing Again.* In it I weave stories with biblical truths about the necessity of wearing the helmet of hope.

There are times when I use the seer gifting that I can perceive people's helmets sitting on the floor, right next them, allowing their minds to be bombarded by the onslaught of the accuser of the brethren. In that moment, I often need to stop, exhort, and remind the group to put back on their helmet of hope and believe that something good is just about to happen!

The Sword of the Spirit

Ephesians 6:17 provides the last piece of armor: "the sword of the Spirit, which is the word of God." The sword (*machaira*) Paul would have been familiar with was a short sword, twelve to fourteen inches in length with a pinpoint tip, able to cut in any direction.

There is one thing that distinguishes the sword from the other five pieces of God's armor that we have examined. The sword is not purely defensive; it is also an offensive weapon. Without it, we have no way to drive off the devil. If we put on all the other armor, we may be able to prevent the devil from wounding us, but we cannot drive him from our presence. Only the sword—the two-edged sword, which is the Word of God—can destroy the devil.

There are two terms in the New Testament for the word *word*. The word used in Ephesians 6:17 does not refer to the Word of Life of 1 John 1:1—the *logos* or written Word; it is not a direct reference to Jesus Christ. The Greek word used to describe the sword of the Spirit here is *rhema*, God's spoken word, His living voice that we hear in our spirits.

It is significant that the sword of the Spirit is not the Bible on a bookshelf or on a nightstand. The actual book with a cover and pages does not scare the devil. But when you read and absorb the Scripture into your heart—and out of the abundance of your heart, your mouth speaks—you have a speech-activated Kingdom. When you quote it directly, it becomes an activated sword wielded by you, empowered by the Holy Spirit.

There are three ways we can wield the sword of the Spirit:

1. We proclaim the Word as Jesus did (see Matthew 4:1–10; Revelation 12).

2. We pray the Bible, the Word of God (see Ephesians 6:18–19; Acts 6:4).

3. We praise with the Word—sing and shout the Scriptures in exaltation of His great name (see Exodus 15:2; 2 Samuel 22:1; Psalm 28:7; Matthew 28:8).

As we conclude this section on the armor of God, it's important to note that there's not one piece of armor you can do without. You can't decide not to wear the belt of truth one day, or forget to put on the breastplate of righteousness, or leave the sword of the Spirit at the Bible study. Every piece of the armor is for your good and God wants you to use it all.

Get ready! Get dressed! You were born in a battle, and you were born to triumph!

FOR REFLECTION AND PRAYER

- How can the shoes of peace make you ready to share the Gospel of peace with a peaceful spirit?
- What are the enemy's most effective flaming arrows to shoot at you, and how can you use the shield of faith to quench them?
- What is the most effective way for you to plant God's thoughts into your mind as you wear the helmet of salvation?

Take a few moments right now to talk to God about the armor He has provided and your desire to wear every piece every day.

VICTORIOUS SPIRITUAL WARFARE PRAYER

Father in heaven, hallowed be Your great name. You are the Almighty God and Your Son is my victorious Champion. I magnify Your great name. You alone are worthy of my praise. You are the Man of War who has triumphed over the powers of darkness. Jesus Christ will return as my victorious Warrior with a two-edged sword in His mouth. Praise You, Lord!

As a warrior in the strategic purposes of God in my generation, I put on the full armor of God. I clothe myself with the belt of truth and truthfulness. I put on the breastplate of righteousness. I declare that I am ready to declare the Good News of the Gospel of peace, and I walk in the strong authority of Your name, Lord Jesus Christ! I take up the shield of faith, enabling me to extinguish the fiery arrows of the evil one. I put on my helmet of the hope of salvation for such a time as this.

I am now ready to take up the powerful sword of the Spirit, which is Your Word, and I proclaim, "No weapon formed against me will prosper." I proclaim Your Word as Jesus did. I pray the Word as the early apostles did, and praise the Word of God as the disciples did. I am more than a conqueror in Christ Jesus. This is my victorious spiritual warfare declaration for Your glory, oh God. Amen and amen!

God's High Praises in Your Mouth

Enter his gates with thanksgiving and his courts with praise; give thanks to him and praise his name.

Psalm 100:4 NIV

James, a half-brother of Jesus, wrote extensively about the negative power of the tongue. James 3:8–9 (NLT) says, "No one can tame the tongue. It is restless and evil, full of deadly poison. Sometimes it praises our Lord and Father, and sometimes it curses those who have been made in the image of God." James said the tongue is "a flame of fire" that "can set your whole life on fire" (verse 6). We must pay great attention to what comes out of our mouths!

But the psalms of David speak of the positive power of what comes out of our mouths. The praises of God in our mouths and His weapons in our hands can deliver a defeating blow to the enemy. Look at what Psalm 149:7–9 says:

> Let the praises of God be in their mouths, and a sharp sword in their hands—to execute vengeance on the nations and punishment on the peoples, to bind their kings with shackles and their leaders with iron chains, to execute the judgment written against them. This is the glorious privilege of his faithful ones.

In the final chapters of part 2 on our spiritual weapons, let's consider and put into practice the power of God that comes through our mouths when we praise, worship, and give thanks. Remember, it's a speech-activated Kingdom!

18

Inspiration from Joshua and Jonah

A human shout is powerful, and we can use a raised voice to communicate a variety of messages: joy, panic or great distress, triumph, intense passion, anger, and excitement. But even more powerful than a shout driven by human effort is a shout that is filled with faith and anointed with praise.

Probably the most famous strategic shout in the Bible is found in Joshua 6. But maybe even just as important as the shout itself was what came before the shout: a fast of silence.

A Fast from Negative Words

Moses, the great deliverer who led all of Israel out of Egypt, had died, and Joshua was now to lead the Israelites to conquer their Promised Land. Jericho was a wall-protected formidable city and Israel's first big challenge under new leadership. Joshua and his army did not know how to make entry into the city, and they were literally up against a wall, but the Lord told Joshua the way:

> Now Jericho [a fortified city with high walls] was tightly closed because [of the people's fear] of the sons of Israel; no one went out

or came in. The Lord said to Joshua, "See, I have given Jericho into your hand, with its king and the mighty warriors. Now you shall march around the city, all the men of war circling the city once. You shall do this [once each day] for six days. Also, seven priests shall carry seven trumpets [made] of rams' horns ahead of the ark; then on the seventh day you shall march around the city seven times, and the priests shall blow the trumpets. When they make a long blast with the ram's horn, and when you hear the sound of the trumpet, all the people shall cry out with a great shout (battle cry); and the wall of the city will fall down in its place, and the people shall go up, each man [going] straight ahead [climbing over the rubble]."

Joshua 6:1–5 AMP

Joshua and his men followed the Lord's directions and marched around the city—silently, doing the impossible by taming the tongue. They did so on the first day, second day, third day, and fourth day. A miracle was already transpiring. I'm sure by the fifth day they were quite tired, perhaps perspiring in the heat of the day as they were trudging around the city walls in utter silence.

But on the seventh day they had different instructions. There is no doubt that a lot of pent-up frustration was brewing—in their persistent silence. After marching around the city one time each of the previous six days, they were to march around the city seven entire times while priests blew rams' horns. At the end of the seventh march around the city, the people were told to shout in unison—and did they ever. They gave the loudest victory shout of their lives, and the impenetrable walls crumbled in the sight of everyone!

Have you considered that part of the victory of the battle of Jericho was that they fasted from grumbling, complaining, and negative speech for seven days? And then they released a united shout of pure praise, glorifying God. It's no wonder that God moved in a supernatural way! There is a behind-the-scenes principle involved here. Sacrifice releases the power of God!

At times over the years, I have challenged people to wear a rubber band around their wrist for seven days; in fact, I have a rubber band around my wrist right now as I compose this chapter. For seven days, when they realize they are being negative, complaining, or grumbling, they are to snap the rubber band on their wrist—just enough to get their attention. Then as a reminder say, "I will not enter His gates or presence with grumbling, complaining, or comparing myself to others. I will enter with thanksgiving and high praise!"

In this season of my life, I need to go on a Jericho fast once again—to remove negativity and replace it with a garment of praise for the Lord. The fast of grumbling and complaining can be intense, but ever so freeing in the arena of spiritual warfare. Will you join me?

Shouting from the Belly of a Whale

Many people believe the story of Jonah in the Bible is a myth. But Jonah was a real prophet who really got swallowed by a very large fish—and lived to pass his dramatic life narrative on to others. The Lord directly told him, "Arise, go to Nineveh, the great city, and cry out against it, because their wickedness has come up before Me" (Jonah 1:2). What did Jonah do after hearing from God? "Jonah got up to flee or run away and head towards Tarshish from the presence of the Lord. So he went down to Joppa, found a ship that was going to Tarshish, paid the fare, and boarded it to go with them to Tarshish away from the presence of the Lord" (Jonah 1:3).

God told Jonah to preach to the people in Nineveh, but something within Jonah resisted the call. He flat out did not want to go, so he ran away from God and disobeyed His word. We will see how Jonah's disobedience to God's voice caused him to fall step by step progressively lower, physically and spiritually. Jonah went from the mountain to the seashore, and from the seashore to a ship. Then what happened? The Bible says that God "hurled a powerful wind over the sea, causing a violent storm that threatened to break the ship apart" (1:4 NLT).

The crew threw Jonah overboard, and he sank even lower—this time into the sea. When we are disobedient, we keep falling. Now in the sea, Jonah descended lower yet:

> So they picked up Jonah and hurled him into the sea, and the sea stopped its raging. Then the men became extremely afraid of the Lord, and they offered a sacrifice to the Lord and made vows. And the Lord designated a great fish to swallow Jonah, and Jonah was in the stomach of the fish for three days and three nights.
>
> Jonah 1:15–17

Jonah was inside a fish for three days and three nights—all because he didn't respond to the Lord's call to preach repentance to the people of Nineveh. What did Jonah do next?

> From inside the fish Jonah prayed to the Lord his God. He said: "*In my distress I called to the Lord*, and he answered me. From deep in the realm of the dead *I called for help*, and *you listened to my cry*. You hurled me into the depths, into the very heart of the seas, and the currents swirled about me; all your waves and breakers swept over me. I said, 'I have been banished from your sight; yet I will look again toward your holy temple.' The engulfing waters threatened me, the deep surrounded me; seaweed was wrapped around my head. To the roots of the mountains I sank down; the earth beneath barred me in forever. But you, Lord my God, brought my life up from the pit. When my life was ebbing away, I remembered you, Lord, and my prayer rose to you, to your holy temple. Those who cling to worthless idols turn away from God's love for them. But *I, with shouts of grateful praise, will sacrifice to you*. What I have vowed I will make good. I will say, 'Salvation comes from the Lord.'" And the Lord commanded the fish, and it vomited Jonah onto dry land.
>
> Jonah 2 NIV, emphasis added

When Jonah finally shouted praises to God in the belly of the fish—when Jonah finally offered thanksgiving while smelling all that was digesting in the belly of the fish—God commanded the fish to expel Jonah onto the shore.

Let's look at this story through the lens of spiritual warfare. Imagine old Jonah in the belly of the sea monster marinating in all kinds of intestinal juices with seaweed wrapped around his head. He is as low as he has ever been in his life.

As the sea monster swims deeper into the sea, Jonah sits, tries to stand, and rolls around inside the behemoth. Jonah finally gets so desperate that with few options left, he starts praising the Lord.[1] The creature suddenly hears from its Creator to head toward the water's surface. As Jonah continues to praise, the spiritual atmosphere changes from as low it can get to something higher—something heavenly. The whale reaches the surface and swims toward the shore. There God says, "Hey, you sea monster, I have a ministry for you. How about throwing up this guy onto the beach? How would you like to be an instrument of deliverance?" And out comes Jonah.

After three days and nights inside a fish, Jonah is covered with seaweed, dripping with green bile, and now plastered with sand. But Jonah picks himself up, perhaps washes himself off, and filled with passion and the word of the Lord heads straight to Nineveh—not planning to disobey this time. No, sir! He points his boney finger at the people and delivers God's message. And a city of more than 120,000 people accepts Jonah's word and repents!

The key principle in both epic stories—Jericho's tumbling walls and Jonah's tumbling fall—is that praise precedes the breakthrough. Will you also shout-praise your way to your breakthrough?

―――――――― FOR REFLECTION AND PRAYER ――――――――

- How often do you notice yourself complaining with negative words coming out of your mouth?

- When is the last time you found yourself sinking lower and lower like Jonah until you felt swallowed up by your problems?
- Have you ever shouted to God with a voice of triumph? Give it a try!

Take a few moments right now to talk to God about any walls you want to see fall, and then use the spiritual weapon of praise to begin to speak to the situation that has swallowed you up.

19

The Power of Worship and Thanksgiving

In the final two chapters in this second part of this book on our spiritual weapons, we will look at three aspects of high praises: worship, thanksgiving, and praise. Each contains spiritual power to defeat the enemy. In this chapter let's see how the spiritual power of our words can be released through *worship* and *thanksgiving*.

When you hear someone today say, "Oh, I love worship," they often mean, "I love worship music," "I love the music service at church," or "I love the presence of the Holy Spirit I feel when I worship."

But worship is not primarily about music, singers, or award-winning production—and I live in Nashville, Tennessee. In its purest form by definition, worship is primarily an inner attitude of the heart of bowing down before Him, and then it is exhibited through our physical bodies.

Worship

Biblically speaking, worship means to bow down in your heart in submission to the Lord. Worship is related to acknowledging and honoring God's attributes. Unlike praise or thanksgiving, worship cannot be commanded. We can say to someone, "Stand up, clap your hands, and praise the Lord!" You can also tell someone to give thanks and he can say, "Thank you." But we cannot force anyone to worship God. Why? Worship is a voluntary act of the heart as an act of submission.

One of the most beautiful places to study what worship looks like is in Isaiah 6. Isaiah is, at that point in time, already a prophet who ministered for the Lord. During his encounter with the beauty realm of God, Isaiah had a vision of worship and praise in heaven:

> It was in the year King Uzziah died that I saw the Lord. He was sitting on a lofty throne, and the train of his robe filled the Temple. Attending him were mighty seraphim, each having six wings. With two wings they covered their faces, with two they covered their feet, and with two they flew. They were calling out to each other, "Holy, holy, holy is the Lord of Heaven's Armies! The whole earth is filled with his glory!" Their voices shook the Temple to its foundations, and the entire building was filled with smoke.
>
> Isaiah 6:1–4 NLT

In this passage we see mighty seraphim, a specific category of angels. The seraphs have six wings. Fascinating! With two wings they covered their faces in humility and worship, with two wings they covered their feet in total dependency on God, and with two wings they fly, denoting service. The seraphs called out singing, "Holy, holy, holy."

King David wrote, "Come, let's *worship* and bow down, let's kneel before the Lord our Maker" (Psalm 95:6, emphasis added).

John the Beloved captures the words of Jesus that explain, "God is spirit, and those who *worship* Him must worship in spirit and truth" (John 4:24, emphasis added).

The book of Matthew gives us a glimpse into when the wise men first saw Jesus: "And after they came into the house, they saw the Child with His mother Mary; and *they fell down and worshiped Him*. Then they opened their treasures and presented to Him gifts of gold, frankincense, and myrrh" (Matthew 2:11, emphasis added).

And Paul told the church in Rome, and us, "Therefore I urge you, brothers and sisters, by the mercies of God, to *present your bodies as a living and holy sacrifice*, acceptable to God, which is *your spiritual service of worship*" (Romans 12:1, emphasis added).

Worship is a powerful tool of spiritual warfare. Worship is a humble posture of heart with a fixed attention on the Lord Jesus, and then a follow through of bodily expression to revere His glorious attributes. Worship breaks through the clouds of spiritual darkness and thrusts us into the light of His face. Worship pierces this temporary present darkness and creates openings for manifest presence to coming flooding through.

Thanksgiving

The giving of thanks uses spoken words to express gratitude for what God does and what He has done. Thanksgiving responds to God's goodness.

I love when my family gets together for a meal. We hold hands in a circle and we sing the simple Johnny Appleseed song "The Lord Is Good to Me" with harmonies. That song is so delightful because it thanks God for His goodness, the sun, the rain, and of course, the apple seed! Are you familiar with the song?

Thanksgiving is a direct command of God according to Colossians 3 and 1 Thessalonians 5:

> And let the peace that comes from Christ rule in your hearts. For as members of one body you are called to live in peace. And always be *thankful*. And whatever you do or say, do it as a representative of the Lord Jesus, *giving thanks* through him to God the Father.
>
> Colossians 3:15, 17 NLT, emphasis added

169

Be thankful in all circumstances, for this is God's will for you who belong to Christ Jesus.

1 Thessalonians 5:18 NLT, emphasis added

Being thankful is related to being in God's will—to be thankful in all things. It doesn't say that everything is God's will, but *to be thankful* is always God's will.

Here's what I was taught: Thanksgiving is the railroad track on which to carry the payload of prayer. Thankfulness is necessary to make other forms of prayer effective. For example, Colossians 4:2 says, "Devote yourselves to prayer with an alert mind and a *thankful heart*" (NLT, emphasis added). Thanksgiving is the key to releasing God's supernatural power (see John 6:11, 23; 11:41-44).

And another aspect of thanksgiving is that thanksgiving sets the "seal of approval" as a way of retaining the blessings we have already received from God's goodness. We can look at the story about the ten lepers that Jesus healed. Only one came back and gave thanks, according to Luke 17:12–19:

And as He entered a village, ten men with leprosy who stood at a distance met Him; and they raised their voices, saying, "Jesus, Master, have mercy on us!" When He saw them, He said to them, "Go and show yourselves to the priests." And as they were going, they were cleansed. Now one of them, when he saw that he had been healed, turned back, glorifying God with a loud voice, and he fell on his face at His feet, giving thanks to Him. And he was a Samaritan. But Jesus responded and said, "Were there not ten cleansed? But the nine—where are they? Was no one found who returned to give glory to God, except this foreigner?" And He said to him, "Stand up and go; your faith has made you well."

All ten received a healing of being cleansed from the dreadful disease of leprosy. Out of the ten, one turned around and gave thanks for what some might consider a partial healing. Jesus was shocked that only one returned to give glory to God. In response,

Jesus declared wholeness to the one who was grateful. One out of the ten then received a miracle as he responded with gratefulness. Are you grateful for the partial? This is another major key in our personal journey of spiritual warfare.

The third aspect of high praises is actually praise itself, which we'll look at next.

FOR REFLECTION AND PRAYER

- Worship is physically bowing in submission to and adoration of the Lord. What does this definition mean to you personally? How can you incorporate into your worship routinely bowing down?
- Thankfulness is necessary to make prayer effective. When do you find yourself the most thankful, and when do you find it a struggle?

Say a prayer of thanks to God for everything you can think of—big and small. Then honor Him in worship, bowing your heart and body before Him for His goodness in your life.

20

THE WEAPON OF PRAISE

Praise is a powerful weapon underutilized today in the Body of Christ. Like worship and thanksgiving, praise comes out of your mouth. But unlike worship, praise can be commanded. There is also a difference between praise and thanksgiving. We praise God for who He is, but thanksgiving is according to what He has done. Praise is related to God's greatness. Psalm 48:1 says, "Great is the Lord, and greatly to be praised."

Seven Scriptural Facts about Praise

1. Praise is a place of God's residence

Psalm 22:3 reveals, "You [God] are enthroned upon the praises of Israel." God is holy. He cannot dwell in an unholy place, and praise sanctifies an atmosphere. This is why you can enter into someone's home and it feels "light." We sense something and think, *Wow, this feels like a place where the Holy Spirit dwells. I wonder why? Could it be that the people here worship and praise the Lord?*

God's address is PRAISE. When you praise God—even in your dungeon, even during your fiery trial—God establishes a throne from which He will rule over your circumstance. He is a territorial God. (We get more into that topic in the chapter on spiritual mapping.)

2. Praise is the way into God's presence

Psalm 100:4 tells us the way into God's presence is by entering "His gates with thanksgiving, and His courtyards with praise." Isaiah 60:18 tells us the entrance as well: "You will call your walls salvation, and your gates praise." One of the gateways into the city of God is called the gate of praise. You can establish a gate of praise into your own home and your own life, which will lead you to the place where God resides.

3. Our praise allows God to bless us

God intervened in King David's situations so David could praise Him. David wrote, "You have turned my mourning into dancing for me; You have untied my sackcloth and encircled me with joy, that my soul may sing praise to You and not be silent. Lord my God, I will give thanks to You forever" (Psalm 30:11–12).

We also see in Psalm 67 how David tied praise to God's blessing. David repeated three times in this psalm, "May the nations praise you." Verses 4 and 5 show the result: "Then the earth will yield its harvests, and God, our God, will richly bless us. Yes, God will bless us, and people all over the world will fear him." This is so powerful! Our praise leads to blessing, which leads to people all over the world fearing the Lord. Our tongue is an instrument of glory, and whatever we sow in rejoicing and praise, we reap God's blessings in return.

4. Praise is a spiritual garment

Isaiah 61:3 (NIV) says there is "a garment of praise instead of a spirit of despair." What is dark, gloomy, and negative can be exchanged for what is beautiful, glorious, and uplifting. When Jesus went into the synagogue in Nazareth, He read this passage from Isaiah as a reference to Himself (see Luke 4:18–19). We can see more closely from Luke that to some degree our deliverance depends upon us casting off the spirit of heaviness and putting on the mantle of praise.

Rather than wearing a garment of negativity, complaints, "what ifs," bitter judgments, and perpetual comparisons, you could be wearing a garment of praise. Even if you have to crowbar yourself out of that pessimistic cloak, do it. It's a mindset that must be changed; it's a stronghold.

Keep that garment on by telling yourself as often as need be: "I am secure in God's love for me. I will bless and not curse. I will not covet. I will forgive. I will even do as Job says and 'rejoice in unsparing pain'" (Job 6:10; also see Psalm 15:4). Deliverance sometimes depends upon us, and you must praise your way out of the stronghold on your life.

Isaiah 52:1–2 tells us, the Church, to wake up and clothe ourselves with strength and beautiful clothes. We are to sit up and shake off the dust of oppression, condemnation, and fear and free ourselves from the chains of bondage and unbelief. We can do that through praise and be refreshed with His goodness.

5. Praise is the means of deliverance

Psalm 50:23 (AMP) says, "Who offers a sacrifice of praise and thanksgiving honors Me; and to him who orders his way rightly [who follows the way that I show him], I shall show the salvation of God." When we praise God amid a terrible situation, salvation and deliverance begin to enter in. Your deliverance may not be sudden or instant, but it will begin. Remember what happened when Jonah, in the belly of the fish, began to offer praises. The fish started moving toward the shore.

We also see in Acts 16:25–26 how praise in the middle of the night opened the doors and loosed the bonds to set Paul and Silas free. Praise silences the devil. Psalm 8:2 (NIV) says: "Through the praise of children and infants you have established a stronghold against your enemies, to silence the foe and the avenger." Because of our spiritual enemies, God has ordained praise so we can silence Satan.

Our mouths are spiritual weapons for both good and evil. Proverbs 18:21 in the Old Testament and James 3:8 in the New Testament both emphasize that death and life are in the power of the tongue. We need to sanctify our lips and learn to use our speech as effective tools of building up and releasing words of edification. We must yield our tongue as an instrument of blessing. Praise is a childlike expression of faith in a complicated world, and praise is a way into our triumph in Christ!

6. Praise is a sacrifice

As mentioned previously, according to Jeremiah 33:11 (NKJV), a sacrifice costs us something. We do not necessarily praise because we feel like it, but because of what God has already done for us. Praise is the voice of the earthly Bride offering a thank offering to her heavenly Bridegroom.

Hebrews 13:15–16 (NIV) describes three sacrifices that we are to offer God through Jesus: Praise, the fruit of our lips that openly profess His name; doing good, the working out of the fruit of the Spirit; and sharing material goods, the fruit of our labor.

7. Praise is lifting holy hands toward God in heaven

This last scriptural fact about the weapon of praise is more like the mechanics or the way to praise the Lord. Psalm 63:3–4 tells us: "Because Your favor is better than life, My lips will praise You. So I will bless You as long as I live; I will lift up my hands in Your name." And 1 Timothy 2:8–9 (NLT) says, "In every place of worship, I want men to pray with holy hands lifted up to God, free from anger and controversy." Yes, lifting holy hands as an act of praising God is a physical expression of praise. But it is our enjoining with other believers that makes it an actual external offering with internal benefits. Remember, praise can be commanded, but worship is an internal act of submission. Psalm 141:2 reveals that our praise goes up to the nostrils of God. David writes: "Let my prayer be set before You as incense, the lifting up of my hands as the evening sacrifice."

For the more exuberant praisers, let's look at Psalm 149:3: "They shall praise His name with dancing; they shall sing praises to Him with tambourine and lyre." And Psalm 150:4: "Praise Him with tambourine and dancing; praise Him with stringed instruments and flute." Dancing is used to show gratitude, praise, and worship to God. We are to express ourselves physically when we praise the Lord!

When, How, and Who to Praise

Lastly, let's look at when, how, and who to praise.

When should we praise God?

King David the psalmist tells us when he will praise God:

> I will exalt you, my God the King; *I will praise your name for ever and ever*. Every day I will praise you and extol your name for ever and ever. Great is the Lord and most worthy of praise; his greatness no one can fathom. My mouth will speak in praise of the Lord. Let every creature praise his holy name *for ever and ever*.
>
> Psalm 145:1–3, 21 NIV, emphasis added

When should we praise? Every day, forever. Psalm 34:1 says, "I will praise the Lord at all times. I will *constantly* speak his praises" (NLT, emphasis added).

How should we praise the Lord?

Wholeheartedly! Psalm 111:1 (NKJV) says, "Praise the Lord! I will praise the Lord with my whole heart." We must praise God knowing what we are doing, with skill: "For God is the King of all the earth; sing praises in a *skillful* psalm and with understanding" (Psalm 47:7 AMP, emphasis added).

Praising God with singing or speaking should be done with excellence unto our Lord and Savior. Psalm 63:4–5 tells us, "I will praise you as long as I live, and in your name I will *lift up my hands*. I will be fully satisfied as with the richest of foods; *with singing lips* my mouth will praise you." We see that we should praise the Lord physically, using our bodies. What better way to use our hands and lips than to praise the Lord?

Who should praise the Lord?

This is a very interesting question. Let's continue in the book of Psalms to answer it: "Everything that has breath shall praise the Lord" (Psalm 150:6). Psalm 148:2–12 (NIV) gives an exhaustive list of who should praise God—seven are listed in heaven and twenty-three on earth are called to praise God:

> Praise him, all his angels; praise him, all his heavenly hosts. Praise him, sun and moon; praise him, all you shining stars. Praise him, you highest heavens and you waters above the skies. Let them praise the name of the Lord, for at his command they were created, and he established them for ever and ever—he issued a decree that will never pass away. Praise the Lord from the earth, you great sea creatures and all ocean depths, lightning and hail, snow and clouds, stormy winds that do his bidding, you mountains and all hills, fruit trees and all cedars, wild animals and all cattle, small creatures and flying birds, kings of the earth and all nations, you princes and all rulers on earth, young men and women, old men and children.

Now, who *cannot* praise the Lord? Psalm 115:17 (NLT) says, "The dead cannot sing praises to the Lord." So, "Everything that has breath shall praise the Lord" (Psalm 150:6). We are to praise the Lord by every means available, whether by ancient and historical ways with the shofar and lyre, or by the latest state-of-the-art means such as podcasts and high-tech digital tools.

We need to be careful, however, not to attempt to replace personally spoken praise with high-tech devices. High tech has no breath. No matter how wonderful the artists or the bands, no matter how pure the sound on the recording technology, God never meant for recordings to be used as a substitute for our own personal praise.

Singing your praises may not sound as professional or as melodic as the praise from artists who write brilliant lyrics and create fresh melodies—which I do love—but there is something very powerful and irreplaceable about praising God for yourself.

God expects and deserves the high praises that come from our own mouths. Praising God brings Him glory and empowers you to secure victory in every battle. Of all the weapons we have discussed, praise ranks as one of the most lethal weapons and expressions of spiritual warfare. It can place principalities in chains (see Psalm 149).

In praise we simply declare what is already written in the Word of God, "It is finished." The great war between Christ and Satan, between good and evil, has already been decided at the cross. God disarmed all the satanic forces by the death and the resurrection of the Lord Jesus Christ. And when we praise Him, we enforce and extend the victory already won at Calvary. This is an honor given to all His godly ones.

FOR REFLECTION AND PRAYER

- How do you express your praise to God? How often do you express your praise bodily?
- If praise is one of the most lethal weapons and expressions of spiritual warfare, how can you incorporate praise more often in response to battles against evil?

Take a few moments to give your praise vocally and physically to God.

Victorious Spiritual Warfare Prayer

I praise You, Lord! Let Your praise be continually on my lips. Every day, forever and ever, I want to praise You. Like the blind man Bartimaeus, I cast off the garments of my old ways and lifestyle. I toss away my grumbling and complaining and I come running to You, my Lord Jesus Christ. I cast off the garments of heaviness and put on new garments of praise. What a glorious exchange. Hallelujah! I declare that You, God, are at residence within my praises. I enter Your presence with my highest praises to You, which You in turn use as a tool to bless me.

In this moment, I put on the whole armor of God, remembering every piece. I put on the belt of truth, the breastplate of righteousness, the shoes fitted with readiness to share the Gospel of peace, the shield of faith, the helmet of salvation that gives me hope, and the sword of the Spirit. I combine this armor with the weapons of praise, thanksgiving, and worship. I join the choirs of angels and I stand with the great cloud of witnesses to proclaim the wonders of God. Together we make up a symphony of praise exalting God Almighty, declaring, "All praise and glory and honor and power be unto the Lamb forever and ever." Amen and amen!

PART 3

ENFORCING CHRIST'S VICTORY

God's Powerful Names

> Therefore God exalted him to the highest place and gave him *the name that is above every name*, that at *the name of Jesus* every knee should bow, in heaven and on earth and under the earth, and every tongue acknowledge that Jesus Christ is Lord, to the glory of God the Father.
>
> Philippians 2:9–11 NIV, emphasis added

What's in a name? A name can release identity, reveal character traits, and carry weighty genealogical heritage. Names are very important. If you have children, do you remember the joy, the delight, and the laboring over what to call or name your child? Especially your first born? I am a father of four and at the time of this writing I am "Opa" or a grandfather to eleven grandchildren. Each child is special, and Michal Ann and I chose each of our children's names with great care, so much pondering, and even more prayer.

A name can tell us who a child's father is. For example, last names such as Johnson and Peterson came from someone being the son of John or the son of Peter. A person's surname or last name has in the past reflected a person's occupation (Baker, Fisher, or Smith) or geographical location (Hill, Stone, or Wood). Now listen to this one. I have a grandson who is the fifth male to carry the same name. You heard me! And for three generations a Goll male has been honored with the middle name Wayne.

God thinks very highly of names and family heritage. Both the Old and New Testaments have genealogies and accounts of family history. When it comes to spiritual warfare, one name rises to the top: Jesus. Every follower of Jesus is called to represent the full authority of that revered, all-powerful name. As we kick off part 3 of this book, we must clearly understand that victory in spiritual warfare is assured because of the triumphant name of Jesus. Without the name of Jesus, no stronghold or demon will budge and we remain afflicted by the enemy. But with the name of Jesus? Well, let's look at this section's theme Scripture passage as stated in the Amplified Bible:

> For this reason also [because He obeyed and so completely humbled Himself], God has highly exalted Him and bestowed on Him the name which is above every name, so that at the name of Jesus every knee shall bow [in submission], of those who are in heaven and on earth and under the earth, and that every tongue will confess and openly acknowledge that Jesus Christ is Lord (sovereign God), to the glory of God the Father.

At some point in time, whether in a millennial reign, after a millennial reign, or in eternity, every knee—*every* knee—will bow and declare verbally that Jesus Christ is Lord. Oh my, what a day it will be when the gods of every Eastern religion; every principality, power, or territorial spirit; every imam or spiritual leader; every "ism"—humanism, communism, and popularity-ism; every diva, influencer, or leader on earth; every philosophy; and every tongue that exalts itself against the knowledge of Christ bow in submission to Him. *Lord, we are excited to peer into Your powerful names and how we can work with You to defeat every enemy of the cross. In Yeshua Jesus' mighty name, amen and amen.*

21

WHAT IS HIS NAME?

In one season of my life and ministry, I had the experience of being cut off from others I had walked with in my personal Christian experience and ministry. I was put on a "blacklist" at one point by a national spiritual leader as someone not to associate with. Sounds like the way the mafia works instead of the way the Body of Christ is supposed to function. It was quite painful and very hard. I felt betrayed, forgotten, and my name no longer seemed to carry the same level of respect and integrity that it had in the past. I understood in part what it is like to feel shunned and disowned.

I believe in God's redemptive plan, but jealousy, bitter root judgments, and other spiritual forces can be used or even permitted to test us by stripping away any identification we might have in a name, gifts, or a ministry. We might find ourselves so pruned back to where what is left is only *en Christos*—a synonym for *Christian* that Paul used in Romans 16:7.

Followers of Jesus Christ were first called Christians in the city of Antioch (see Acts 11:26). The term was probably not a compliment, but it was the name that quickly became connected to those who claimed to belong to Christ. When someone asks you about your faith, do you proudly say, "I'm a Christian," or have you been so embarrassed at the poor behavior of other Christians that you hesitate to identify as a Christian?

We must never be ashamed to identify as someone who is a Christian—someone in Christ following the teachings and life example of Jesus. In spiritual warfare, we must find our identity in Him and Him alone. It is only at His name that every knee bows.

As you study the names of God in the next two chapters and bask in the reality that He has given you His name, I pray you will be overcome in worship for Him. In His name is all authority, power, provision, identity, security, and relationship with Almighty God. Wear His name with honor. Declare His name to the ends of the earth. Stake your all in His name. Live worthy of His name. Boast in His name for His name is great and greatly to be praised.

Who Do You Say I Am?

Who do you say Jesus is? That is a huge question that has to be answered by each person. Let's look at this question of identity. When Jesus and His disciples reached the district of Caesarea in Philippi, Jesus asked them, "Who do people say the Son of Man is?" (Matthew 16:13 NIV). They told Jesus that some believed he was John the Baptist, Elijah, Jeremiah, or another prophet.

Jesus then penetratingly personalized the question:

> "But who do *you yourselves* say that I am?" Simon Peter answered, "You are the Christ, the Son of the living God." And Jesus said to him, "Blessed are you, Simon Barjona, because flesh and blood did not reveal this to you, but My Father who is in heaven."
>
> Matthew 16:15–17, emphasis added

The Spirit of the Lord came upon this natural man, Peter, and a revelation was given to him that Jesus was the Messiah. Overfamiliarity can block you from knowing who Christ is. Overfamiliarity can be a demonic weapon that keeps people from recognizing their destiny by not acknowledging who Jesus really is: Christ, the Son of the living God.

Who is this Man named Jesus? What are His claims? What did He do? What does He do today? As it was at that literal moment when Jesus asked His disciples, so it is today. It takes God to know who God is. It takes the ministry of the Holy Spirit to reveal to us who this glorious Man Christ Jesus really is and who He is in us.

I Am Who I Am

Moses was confronted with a similar question when he was sent to deliver the children of Israel from Egypt. Exodus 3:13–14 describes an intriguing discussion between God and Moses:

> Then Moses said to God, "Behold, I am going to the sons of Israel, and I will say to them, 'The God of your fathers has sent me to you.' Now they may say to me, 'What is His name?' What shall I say to them?" And God said to Moses, "I AM WHO I AM"; and He said, "This is what you shall say to the sons of Israel: 'I AM has sent me to you.'"

Moses was familiar with the Egyptian tradition of naming every god, so he was naturally anticipating the question, "What is His name?" He was asking ahead of time to be prepared for what was coming. God's response was, "I AM WHO I AM." He was saying, "I am the Self-Existent One; the Eternal One; the One who always has been and always will be." God's response was equivalent to saying, "I am Jehovah the Eternal."

Never in the Bible has God described or named Himself, "I WAS." No, never! He is the God of today. He is present tense all the time "I AM." We too often dwell in the past. He is the God of today. He is Jehovah now. He is the Great I AM, always ready to

189

come to our aid with more than enough love, power, and resources. This is why God told Moses to tell the Israelites, "I AM has sent me to you."

Over the past years, many have taught about the compound names of God from the Old Testament. There is a revelation in every name:

- He is Jehovah *Nissi*—the Lord Our Banner (Exodus 17:15).
- He is Jehovah *Tsidkenu*—the Lord Is Our Righteousness (Jeremiah 23:6).
- How wonderful it is that He is our Jehovah *Shalom*—the Lord Is Peace (Judges 6:24).
- He is Jehovah *Rophe*—the Lord Who Heals (Exodus 15:22–26).
- He reveals Himself as our Jehovah *M'Kaddesh*—the Lord Who Sanctifies (Leviticus 20:8).
- Consider the meaning of Jehovah *Shammah*—the Lord Is There (Ezekiel 48:35).
- The name Jehovah *Jireh* tells us—the Lord Will Provide (Genesis 22:14).
- He is Jehovah *Rohi*—the Lord Our Shepherd (Psalm 23:1).

What is His name? I hope you are seeing that God has many names that each reveal another aspect of His multifaceted character, personality, and nature. The names of Jesus are many, and there is power in each one, which leads to our triumph in Christ.

FOR REFLECTION AND PRAYER

- If someone were to ask you, "Who do you say that Jesus is?" how would you reply?

- Which of the eight compound names of God used in the Old Testament have special meaning to you? Why?

Take a few moments right now to talk to God using one of His compound names, thanking Him for the trait that name exemplifies.

22

THE NAMES OF JESUS FROM GENESIS TO REVELATION

The names of Jesus are like spiritual jackhammers, and using them in spiritual warfare is a strategic way to enforce Christ's victory. They also break up anything we have leaned on other than Jesus alone for security or identity. The jealousy of God is not satisfied until the identities of His special names are placed deep within our own identities—until we find our total security and identity only in Him.

In chapter two I listed 50 of the 140 powerful names of God found throughout Scripture. In this chapter I'm going to give you all 140 with brief commentary on each. I urge you not to skip over these names. Each name reveals an aspect of the character and the nature of the Son of God. Read each deliberately and let the Holy Spirit reveal to you who Jesus is by His names. Then pray these names according to the Scriptures. I encourage you to use this as a special study guide to discover your answer to Jesus' question, "Who do you say I am?" (Matthew 16:15 NIV).

Will you pray this with me? "Holy Spirit, reveal the glorious Son of God as I meditate on Your names."

1. Seed of the woman (Genesis 3:15). The first mention of a Redeemer, the first of many prophecies regarding the Messiah.

2. Jehovah, the Lord (Genesis 19:24; Psalm 110:1, 5). Jehovah, the true God, Creator of everything.

3. Shiloh (Genesis 49:10). Shiloh is used thirty-two times in the Old Testament referring to the Messiah as well as to a location.

4. The Star from Jacob (Numbers 24:17). Jesus is the Star who came from the lineage of Jacob, bringing salvation to the world.

5. Prophet (Deuteronomy 18:15; Luke 24:19). Jesus as the Prophet is prophesied in the Old Testament and proven true in the New Testament.

6. Rock of Salvation (Deuteronomy 32:15). This name signifies a sense of security and strength.

7. Daysman (Job 9:33 KJV). A daysman is an umpire, arbiter, or mediator.

8. God's Anointed (Psalm 2:2). God's Chosen One.

9. Son (Psalm 2:12; Hebrews 3:6). Again, God's Chosen One.

10. Sanctuary (Isaiah 8:14). Jesus is a refuge, a shelter for His followers.

11. Stone of Stumbling (Isaiah 8:14). For others He will cause them to stumble and fall.

12. Rock of Offense (Isaiah 8:14). For others He will cause offense.

13. Wonderful (Isaiah 9:6 NKJV). The Wonderful Counselor.

14. Counselor (Isaiah 9:6 NKJV). The Counselor who is wonderful.

15. Mighty God (Isaiah 9:6 NKJV). Superhuman hero of the people.

16. Everlasting Father (Isaiah 9:6 NKJV). Father of eternity.

17. Prince of Peace (Isaiah 9:6 NKJV). Royalty bringing peace to all who receive Him.

18. Root of Jesse (Isaiah 11:10). The Messiah came from the root, the family tree, of Jesse who was King David's father.

19. Branch (Isaiah 11:1; Zechariah 3:8; 6:12). The Branch is Jesus who grew out of the stem of Jesse.

20. Banner to the People (Isaiah 11:10 NKJV). Jesus will be raised high as a rallying banner for the people.

21. God's Servant (Isaiah 42:1; Matthew 12:18). Jesus was and is God's servant, obeying His every command and desire.

22. Chosen One (Isaiah 42:1). God selected Jesus as His Son, the beloved Anointed One who pleases the Father.

23. Sharp Sword, Polished Arrow (Isaiah 49:2). God's Word is living and active and brilliant.

24. Redeemer (Isaiah 59:20). The One who saves from danger or destruction, restores rights, and avenges wrongs.

25. Angel of His Presence (Isaiah 63:9). God of patience and gentleness and mercy.

26. Lord Our Righteousness (Jeremiah 23:6). God of holiness, morality, justice, and virtue.

27. Plant of Renown (Ezekiel 34:29 KJV). The Messiah, the Branch from the root of David.

28. Messiah the Prince (Daniel 9:25; John 4:25). The Heir of God's throne and Savior of the people.

29. Judge of Israel (Micah 5:1). The Ruler in Israel.

30. Desire of All Nations (Haggai 2:7 NKJV). Jesus the Messiah; the Savior of every nation.

31. My Associate (Zechariah 13:7). God's Son, Friend, near and dear Beloved.

32. Refiner and Purifier (Malachi 3:3). The One who died to cleanse people of sin to become a righteous offering to the Lord.

33. Sun of Righteousness (Malachi 4:2). The Messiah who ushers in the Day of the Lord with healing in His wings.

34. Jesus Christ (Matthew 1:1 KJV). The one and only Son of God, the Messiah, Savior.

35. Son of Abraham (Matthew 1:1 KJV). The Seed of Abraham in whom all nations of the earth were blessed.

36. Son of David (Matthew 1:1; 9:27 KJV). This name reflects His lineage from Jesse through David.

37. Christ (Matthew 1:17; 2:4 KJV). The Greek word for Christ is *Christos* and the Hebrew word is *Meshiakh*. Both mean "Anointed One."

38. Jesus (Matthew 1:21 KJV). The name the angel of the Lord told Joseph he should name Mary's Child, who was conceived by the Holy Spirit.

39. Emmanuel (God with us) (Matthew 1:23 KJV). The name Joseph was told to name the holy Child.

40. King of the Jews (Matthew 2:2; 21:5). The name the wise men used after being sent by King Herod to find baby Jesus whom he considered a threat to his reign.

41. Governor (Matthew 2:6 KJV). Ruler over and shepherd of God's people.

42. Nazarene (Matthew 2:23). Joseph was told in a dream to take Mary and Jesus to live in Nazareth, hence Jesus became a Nazarene—one who lived in Nazareth.

43. Son of God (Matthew 4:3). The name the devil used when tempting Jesus in the wilderness.

44. Teacher (Matthew 8:19). Jesus taught people about the Kingdom of God wherever He went.

45. The Son of Man (Matthew 8:20). The Hebrew translation of this phrase expresses both the weakness and frailty and the greatness and strength of human nature—representing Jesus in human form.

46. Physician (Matthew 9:12). The divine Doctor who came to heal the sick, the sinners, and the dying.

47. Groom (Matthew 9:15; John 3:29). Jesus is the Bridegroom of His Bride, the Church.

48. Friend of Sinners (Matthew 11:19; Luke 7:34). Jesus ate dinner with tax collectors and others who didn't strictly follow the law. He rejected laws that contradicted God's wisdom and compassion. (I love that song by Casting Crowns, "Jesus, Friend of Sinners," written by Matthew West and Mark Hall. Listen on YouTube.)

49. Beloved (Matthew 12:18; 17:5). This name fulfills the prophecy in Isaiah 42.

50. Sower (Matthew 13:3–9). Jesus is the Sower who came to earth to spread (sow) the Good News of the Kingdom of God. Some of the people who heard the teachings absorbed it and others didn't.

51. Son of the Most High (Luke 1:32). Signifies Christ's divine nature and God's Son.

52. Horn of Salvation (Luke 1:69). Horns are symbolic of power; Jesus is the Power of Salvation for all who accept Him.

53. Dayspring from on High (Luke 1:78 KJV). Dayspring means the rising of the sun, the spring of the day; a metaphor for Jesus the Messiah who brought the world His light that pierces the darkness.

54. Christ the Lord (Luke 2:11). Christ the Lord is the Savior of the world, above all prophets, kings, and priests, the only acceptable sacrifice to God for sin.

55. Savior (Luke 2:11). The Savior came to deliver, preserve, save us, and free us from all evil and danger.

56. Consolation of Israel (Luke 2:25). To console is to remove or alleviate grief, loss, or troubles and comfort and soothe those who are suffering.

57. Salvation (Luke 2:30). Jesus is Salvation because He paid the price for God's children's sins; He is our Savior.

58. Jesus of Nazareth (Luke 4:34). Joseph was told in a dream to take Mary and Jesus to live in Nazareth; hence, Jesus became a Nazarene—one who lived in Nazareth.

59. Holy One of God (Luke 4:34). Even the evil spirits knew that Jesus was God's Son and could not defeat Him.

60. The Word (John 1:1–2). John explained so beautifully that God was Three in One—Father, Son, Holy Spirit—always sharing one nature for eternity.

61. God (John 1:1–3; 20:28; Hebrews 1:8). "Doubting" Thomas identified clearly Jesus as his Lord and his God. He saw and felt proof-positive the places where Jesus was pierced for our sins.

62. True Light (John 1:9). Jesus is the only true and perfect Light of life, wisdom, and love.

63. Only Begotten Son (John 1:18; 3:16 NKJV). We can see God only through His Son, His only Son, Jesus.

64. Lamb of God (John 1:29; Revelation 5:6). When John the Baptist saw Jesus walking toward him, his first words were, "Behold, the Lamb of God!" He knew God's plan was for His Son to be the sacrificial Lamb once and for all.

65. King of Israel (John 1:49). Seven names are used for Jesus in John 1, the King of Israel is one that echoes Isaiah 11:1–2 describing the future King who would have God's spirit of wisdom.

66. Teacher, Rabbi (John 3:2). The name rabbi is a gesture of respect for a teacher of stature.

67. Gift of God (John 4:10). Jesus Himself is the Gift as well as His desire to share the gift of living water to a woman who thirsted for more.

68. Savior of the World (John 4:42). Jesus came not only for the those in Jerusalem, Judea, and Samaria, but also for all people worldwide. He sent His disciples to be witnesses to the end of the earth.

69. Bread of God (John 6:33). This name means Jesus nourishes our physical and spiritual selves from God the Father.

70. Bread of Life (John 6:35, 48–51). Likewise, this name means Jesus feeds life into our bodies and spirits.

71. Light of the World (John 8:12). Jesus declares this name for Himself, saying, "I am the Light of the world." In the Greek, the phrase means He is the single, solitary source of light.

72. Door or Gate of the Sheep (John 10:7). Another declaration from Jesus, this time naming Himself, "I am the door of the sheep." Sheep need to be contained for their safety and well-being. We are His sheep.

73. Good Shepherd (John 10:11). Jesus tells us His name, "I am the good shepherd." He protects us, His sheep, even to the point of dying for us.

74. The Way, the Truth, the Life (John 14:6). We cannot even approach our heavenly Father without first going through Jesus who tells us, "I am the way, and the truth, and the life."

75. The Vine (John 15:1–8). Christians attached to the True Vine will bear fruit, producing evidence of their life in Christ.

76. Lord and God (John 20:28). Although Thomas needed physical proof to call out Jesus as his Lord and God, Jesus says in the next verse, "blessed are those who have not seen and yet believe."

77. Holy and Righteous One (Acts 3:14). This is the name Peter called Jesus when talking to the crowd on the Temple Mount after His crucifixion.

78. Holy Servant Jesus (Acts 4:27). Jesus submitted Himself totally to His Father's plan of redemption, leaving His kingship in heaven to become a holy servant on earth.

79. Prince and Savior (Acts 5:31). The name Prince and Savior accurately describes His role as the King's Son and our Savior.

80. Lord of All (Acts 10:36). Our God shows no favoritism, no partiality, when it comes to His saving grace.

81. Propitiation (Romans 3:25; 1 John 2:2). God offered Christ as a sacrifice of atonement, the propitiation, through His blood shed for us.

82. Christ Jesus our Lord (Romans 6:23). This name comes as a gift from God: "For the wages of sin is death, but the gracious gift of God is eternal life in Christ Jesus our Lord."

83. The Deliverer (Romans 11:26). Jesus will set the captives free—you and me—from ungodliness.

84. Lord Jesus Christ; Christ Jesus (2 Corinthians 1:2; 1 Timothy 2:5). This name brings with it grace and peace from God the Father.

85. The Power of God (1 Corinthians 1:24). All who are called by God receive His power and wisdom.

86. The Wisdom of God (1 Corinthians 1:24). All who are called by God receive His wisdom and power.

87. Sanctification (1 Corinthians 1:30). Because He is Sanctification, we are right with God, pure and holy and free from sin.

88. Lord of Glory (1 Corinthians 2:8). Sin prevented humans from sharing in Christ's glory; after His sacrifice, we can call Him Lord of Glory.

89. Our Passover (1 Corinthians 5:7). Jesus is the Passover Lamb, the One served and sacrificed for us.

90. Spiritual Rock (1 Corinthians 10:4). In Exodus, all God's people ate manna from heaven and drank water from the rock. During communion we eat and drink from the Christ, our Spiritual Rock.

91. Christ the Firstfruits (1 Corinthians 15:23). If Christ was raised as the first of the harvest, then we followers will be raised as well.

92. The Last Adam (1 Corinthians 15:45). Unlike the first Adam who died, the Last Adam, Jesus, lives forever.

93. The Second Man (1 Corinthians 15:45–47). The Second Man, Jesus, came from heaven.

94. Image of God (2 Corinthians 4:4). Christ is the exact likeness of God.

95. Seed of Abraham (Galatians 3:29 KJV). Because Jesus is the Seed of Abraham, we are true children of Abraham, heirs in the Kingdom of God.

96. The Beloved (Ephesians 1:6). Father God's only Son, whom we praise and adore.

97. Chief Cornerstone (Ephesians 2:20 NKJV). In ancient times, the cornerstone was the first rock used to establish a building's foundation. Jesus is the Rock on which we must stand first before all.

98. Head of the Church (Colossians 1:18). As the Church is the Body of Christ, He is the Head.

99. Firstborn from the Dead (Colossians 1:18). A reference to Jesus' resurrection—from death to life.

100. Christ Jesus our Lord (1 Timothy 1:12). The apostle Paul used this name seven times in his writings, perhaps to reflect the significance of Christ as Jesus and Lord.

101. Mediator (1 Timothy 2:4–5). Jesus steps in as every believer's Advocate with the Father.

102. The Man Christ Jesus (1 Timothy 2:5). This is the only Man who can reconcile us with God.

103. Ransom for All (1 Timothy 2:6). His purpose was to sacrifice Himself for all of us.

104. Seed of David (2 Timothy 2:8 NKJV). Jesus fulfilled the prophecy of being a son of David.

105. God the Father and the Lord Jesus Christ our Savior (Titus 1:4 KJV). Number 105 is actually two names. They clearly point to the fact that God the Father and Jesus Christ are part of the Triune Godhead.

106. Blessed Hope (Titus 2:13). The coming appearance of the glory of God is our Blessed Hope, Jesus.

107. Great God and Savior, Jesus Christ (Titus 2:13). This name emphasizes His majesty and magnificence.

108. Radiance of His Glory (Hebrews 1:3). God's divinity revealed brilliantly.

109. Express Image of His Person (Hebrews 1:3 KJV). The exact imprint of God's nature.

110. Upholder of All Things (Hebrews 1:3 KJV). His power is evident universally.

111. Captain of Salvation (Hebrews 2:10 NKJV). The ultimate and eternal Leader.

112. Apostle and High Priest of our Confession (Hebrews 3:1). Jesus replaces the need for an earthy intermediary between us and our heavenly Father.

113. Forerunner (Hebrews 6:20). Jesus has gone ahead of us, preparing the way.

114. Minister in the Sanctuary (Hebrews 8:2). Jesus' superior priesthood is the true and holy tabernacle.

115. Testator (Mediator) of a New Covenant (Hebrews 9:16–17 NKJV). Jesus ushered in the New Covenant by way of His once-and-for-all sacrifice, replacing the need for the Old Covenant's animal offerings.

116. Author and Finisher of Faith (Hebrews 12:2). Jesus is the ultimate fulfillment of God's promises through faith in Him.

117. Great Shepherd of the Sheep (Hebrews 13:20). As elsewhere in the Bible, Jesus' image is a devoted Shepherd providing guidance, protection, and attention.

118. Shepherd and Guardian of Souls (1 Peter 2:25 AMP). A gentle warrior and spiritual gatekeeper of our hearts and souls.

119. Chief Shepherd (1 Peter 5:4). Beyond the shepherd in the field tending to the sheep, the Chief Shepherd, Christ, will return with crowns in hand for His followers.

120. Lord and Savior Jesus Christ (2 Peter 1:11). Believers will be welcomed into the eternal Kingdom of our Lord and Savior Jesus Christ.

121. Day Star (2 Peter 1:19 KJV). Prophecies from God should be taken as a light that shines in the darkness—as a day star rises in your heart.

122. Advocate (1 John 2:1). Jesus is our Attorney, our Mediator who speaks on our behalf before the Father.

123. Jesus Christ the Righteous (1 John 2:1). Emphasizing again that Christ is our Attorney, our Mediator, who speaks on our behalf before the Father.

124. Eternal Life (1 John 5:20). Our assurance of salvation and everlasting life in heaven.

125. Faithful Witness (Revelation 1:5). Jesus is the honest and reliable Source of what John recorded in book of Revelation.

126. Firstborn of the Dead (Revelation 1:5). Jesus rose from the dead in a glorified, eternal body.

127. Ruler of the kings of the earth (Revelation 1:5). When Jesus returns, He will reign and rule over all nations.

128. Alpha and Omega (Revelation 1:8; 21:6; 22:13). Alpha and Omega are the first and last Greek letters in the alphabet. Jesus is the First and the Last.

129. The Beginning and the End (Revelation 1:8 NKJV). Jesus has always existed and will always exist.

130. The First and the Last (Revelation 2:8). Jesus has eternally existed.

131. Morning Star (Revelation 2:28). Jesus, the Morning Star, will appear in the air for all believers in the rapture.

132. The Amen (Revelation 3:14). God's perfect and final revelation.

133. Faithful and True Witness (Revelation 3:14). Jesus never wavers from the whole truth.

134. Origin of Creation (Revelation 3:14; John 1:3; Ephesians 3:9; Colossians 1:15–18). God was and is the Creator of everything.

135. Lion of the Tribe of Judah (Revelation 5:5). Jesus' lineage includes Jacob, whose son was named Judah, a lion's cub, and one of the twelve tribes.

136. The Root of David (Revelation 5:5). Jesus, a member of King David's royal lineage.

137. The Word of God (Revelation 19:13). This name is given to Jesus upon His second coming, claiming victory.

138. King of kings, Lord of lords (Revelation 19:16). Jesus will be accurately named upon His arrival to be declared the Ruler on earth.

139. Root and Offspring of David (Revelation 22:16 KJV). Descendant of King David and Heir.

140. Bright Morning Star (Revelation 22:16; Malachi 4:2). Jesus will appear before the sun rises.

I hope reading these names of God awakened your spirit to know Jesus in a fresh way. I recommend you consider studying these powerful names of God more in depth, and continue to pray over these names and absorb the revelation of Christ into your heart.

Every name contains a distinct revelation of the nature of God Himself. As you pray the names of the Son of God—Jesus Christ our Lord—the Holy Spirit will highlight one of them to you. Then stop. Pause. Selah. Let the power of that name soak deep inside of you, and you will be changed!

FOR REFLECTION AND PRAYER

- Which of the names spoke to you the loudest as you read? Why?
- What aspect of the character or nature of the Son of God stands out to you most? Why?

Take a few moments to pray right now, addressing God using several of His names in this chapter—thanking Him, calling out to Him for help, and strategically using His names against any opposition from the enemy you are facing right now.

VICTORIOUS SPIRITUAL WARFARE PRAYER

My Father, hallowed be Your great and mighty name! Your presence, power, and character are contained within Your glorious names. Thank You for revealing Yourself so completely in Your Word, displaying Your attributes and divine character. Your name shall forever be upon my lips!

With gratitude I passionately proclaim, "I belong to Christ, and I am in Christ." Help me to represent Your name honorably through my attitude and conduct. I prioritize Your name above everything else in my life. I exalt the name of Jesus above my reputation, gifts, anointing, and ministry.

I am excited to learn even more about who You are to me personally, and I will stand in confidence knowing there is one name that is always victorious. I arise in spiritual warfare and exercise the rich and authoritative name of the Lord Jesus Christ. Yes, I stand on solid ground when at the mention of the name of Jesus, demons tremble and dark powers and principalities fall. I am an overcomer in Christ Jesus who is the ultimate King of kings and the Lord of lords. Amen and amen!

CHRIST'S BLOOD SPEAKS

They have defeated him by the blood of the Lamb and by their testimony. And they did not love their lives so much that they were afraid to die.

Revelation 12:11 NLT

If you grew up going to church, you probably received the Lord's Supper or Communion. If so, what is your view about this tradition? More than likely, your church background has shaped your perspective and belief system.

Is Communion solely a way to remember and honor Christ's sacrifice by taking the wafers and juice? If you came from a Catholic or Orthodox tradition, do you believe that the Eucharist is the actual body and blood of Christ? Or do you believe that Christ is present as we gather around the sacraments of His Last Supper even though the bread and wine retain their nature? Regardless of your past or present beliefs, the next three chapters will provide fresh insight into the power of the blood of Jesus and how you can defeat the enemy with the blood of the Lamb.

This section's theme Scripture passage comes from Revelation 12:11 (NASB): "And they," the believers, "overcame him," the accuser, "because of the blood of the Lamb and because of the word of their testimony," what they are testifying about is the issue, "and they did not love their life even when faced with death." Wow! What a powerful combination that leads to overcoming the enemy. And notice a central part of God's overcoming strategy: the blood of Jesus.

I pray that as you begin this section the Spirit of revelation will rest upon you. Where there has been knowledge, there will be an increase of knowledge, and that God will bring you into a place of greater intimacy with Him through studying how Christ's blood *still* speaks.

There is no triumph apart from the blood of Jesus, so these next chapters are vital so you can arm yourself for spiritual warfare.

23

The Power of the Blood in the Old and New Testaments

Blood. What is your first reaction when you read that word? Do you get squeamish? Some people deal with blood every day—surgeons, nurses, first responders, farmers, butchers, and chefs. Women understand that blood is a part of a healthy, monthly cycle. Outside of that, our modern society has almost removed the sight of blood from our daily lives. If you go to a grocery store, you rarely see blood. Meat sellers put special pads under the meat to soak up any blood or juices that might still be present at the time of packaging. But blood has been a regular part of life for most of human history. Life is in the blood, and it's time we knew its power and place more fully.

From Genesis through Revelation, blood takes a central place in the Scriptures. In the Old Testament we see the blood of animals foreshadow the sacrifice of Christ in the New Testament.

Under the Law of Atonement, after the priest had ministered at the altar of incense—past the outer court, the inner court, and the Holy Place, ministering at the fifth station of the altar of incense—he went beyond the veil into the Most Holy Place. Here the priest would take some of the blood of the bull and goat and sprinkle it upon the mercy seat with his finger and on the horns of the altar, seven times each. *Really?* You may be thinking, *Show that to me in the Bible.* Leviticus 16:18–19 specifically states:

> Then he shall go out to the altar that is before the LORD and make atonement for it; he shall take some of the blood from the bull and some of the blood from the goat, and put it on the horns of the altar on all sides. With his finger he shall sprinkle some of the blood on it seven times and cleanse it, and consecrate it from the impurities of the sons of Israel.

When we look closely at all of Leviticus 16, we find that the blood was sprinkled in three distinct locations, seven times each. Some Bible teachers have taught that the three locations pointed to the Godhead, the Trinity, and seven is the number of completion.

This was a picture foreshadowing what was yet to come. When the High Priest, Jesus, shed His blood, He did a complete work one time, for all time and all people. On the cross He said, "It is finished" (John 19:30). The work of atonement was now perfectly accomplished through the blood of this one Man, the Lamb of God, Christ Jesus the Lord!

In the New Testament, the high priest went into the holy of holies only once a year, and that was with the blood of the sacrifice on the most holy day, the Day of Atonement, the Day of Covering.

This sacrifice was a *covering* of sin, but not for the *removal* of sin. There was no access into the presence of God without the shedding of sacrificial blood. This is found and can be studied in Hebrews 9:6–14:

Now when these things have been so prepared, the priests are continually entering the outer tabernacle, performing the divine worship, but into the second, only the high priest enters once a year, not without taking blood which he offers for himself and for the sins of the people committed in ignorance. The Holy Spirit is signifying this, that the way into the holy place has not yet been disclosed while the outer tabernacle is still standing, which is a symbol for the present time. Accordingly both gifts and sacrifices are offered which cannot make the worshiper perfect in conscience, since they relate only to food, drink, and various washings, regulations for the body imposed until a time of reformation.

But when Christ appeared as a high priest of the good things having come, He entered through the greater and more perfect tabernacle, not made by hands, that is, not of this creation; and not through the blood of goats and calves, but through His own blood, He entered the holy place once for all time, having obtained eternal redemption. For if the blood of goats and bulls, and the ashes of a heifer sprinkling those who have been defiled, sanctify for the cleansing of the flesh, how much more will the blood of Christ, who through the eternal Spirit offered Himself without blemish to God, cleanse your conscience from dead works to serve the living God?

I love the phrase, "When Christ appeared." Yes, when Jesus appeared, He offered His blood, which was without blemish, as an eternal sacrifice for our sins.

Seven Ways Christ's Blood Was Shed for Us

Let's look further at how Christ's blood was shed for us so we can feel the depth of His sacrifice and truly cherish the price He paid for our sins. This is the weight behind the power of the blood in spiritual warfare.

1. Jesus sweat drops of blood. Luke 22:44 records, "And being in agony, He was praying very fervently; and His sweat became like drops of blood, falling down upon the ground." In Gethsemane, Jesus was willing to identify Himself with the sin of the world and His capillaries burst. There was such an intensity in His prayer that His blood vessels actually broke and blood flowed in drops of sweat.

2. Jesus bled as He was struck with fists. Matthew 26:59–68 records when Jesus was questioned by Jewish leaders and their volatile response. After the high priest asked the second time if Jesus was the Son of God, Jesus said, "You have said it. And in the future you will see the Son of Man seated in the place of power at God's right hand and coming on the clouds of heaven" (verse 64 NLT). "Then the high priest tore his robes and said, 'He has blasphemed!'" This is a culminating display of agitation and tension. "'What further need do we have of witnesses? See, you have now heard the blasphemy. What do you think?' They answered, 'He deserves death!'" Then the scene turned ugly: "They spit in His face and beat Him with their fists; and others slapped Him." An Old Testament prophecy was fulfilled when the servants struck Him with their fists (see Micah 5:1).

3. Blood spilled when Jesus' beard was ripped off His face. Many centuries before Jesus was born in Bethlehem, Isaiah spoke this Messianic prophecy: "I offered my back to those who beat me, my cheeks to those who pulled out my beard; I did not hide my face from mocking and spitting" (Isaiah 50:6 NIV). Being a man who has had a beard for fifty years, I have a little understanding of the pain involved. But Jesus' beard would have been a long, rough beard that they pulled out with tongs, which more than likely pulled out flesh too, causing the blood to spill out from the wounds.

4. Blood flowed from the flogging of Jesus' back. Matthew 27:26 records, "After having Jesus flogged," which refers to how they scourged His back, "he handed Him over to be crucified." Jesus gave His back to be scourged. Psalm 129:1–3 (AMP) gives a depiction of the raw nature of His treatment: "The [enemies, like] plowers plowed on my back; they made their furrows [of suffering] long."

Have you seen the movie *The Passion of the Christ?* A lot of people could not handle the violent brutality of what happened before and during Christ's crucifixion. When I was watching the movie—and because I have studied these scriptures—I felt the Holy Spirit whisper to me that what was shown in the movie was actually a mild depiction of what Jesus, the Lamb of God, actually went through. I do not believe we can comprehend how disfigured and marred His body became.

5. **Blood streamed down Jesus' face and body from the crown of thorns pressed into His head.** Matthew 27:29 says, "And after twisting together a crown of thorns, they put it on His head, and put a reed in His right hand; and they knelt down before Him and mocked Him saying, 'Hail, King of the Jews!'" This wreath of thorns were long needles placed on His head and then pressed down, pushed down into His scalp, causing streams of blood to pour down over His face and down His back.

Another corresponding Scripture is found in the book of Isaiah. "Just as many were appalled at you, My people, so His appearance was marred beyond that of a man, and His form beyond the sons of mankind" (Isaiah 52:14). Some Bible teachers conclude that the Messiah was horrifically beaten with fists and rods, causing His facial appearance to become so marred that He was totally unrecognizable.

6. **Blood dripped from Jesus' crucified hands and feet.** As recorded in Matthew 27:35 (KJV): "They crucified him, and parted his garments, casting lots: that it might be fulfilled which was spoken by the prophet." They crucified Jesus with a punishment that was not due Him, but that of a criminal, driving nails through His hands and His feet into a wooden cross.

7. **Blood flowed out of Jesus' side when He was pierced.** John, Jesus' beloved disciple who stood next to the cross, wrote that "one of the soldiers pierced Jesus' side with a spear, bringing a sudden

flow of blood and water." (John 19:34 NIV). Even after Jesus had died, a soldier chose to thrust a spear into Jesus' side.

When we can picture how blood—the very life of Jesus—gushed out from His entire body, how can we not bow low in humility and worship Him? We must lift our hands in complete surrender to the One who made such an extravagant sacrifice for us. I encourage you to pause, right now, and take a moment to reflect upon what Jesus did because He loves you. No other love is stronger, and this is the sacrificial love you must remember in spiritual warfare. *Jesus, I honor You. Your sacrifice astounds me. Indeed, Your blood was shed for all mankind. Oh how I love You.*

Seven Benefits of the Blood of Jesus

Seven sprinklings by the high priest and seven piercings by the Messiah bring us seven specific benefits of His spilt blood revealed in Scripture: forgiveness, cleansing, redemption, justification, sanctification, peace, and access. As mentioned previously, according to Revelation 12:11 we have overcome the evil one by testifying what the blood of Jesus has done for us. His triumph over the powers of darkness is enforced as we agree with and declare the benefits of His poured-out blood.

The blood of Jesus leads us to victory in every spiritual battle we face. Leviticus 17:11 declares there is life in the blood. In Christ's blood, we receive life that death cannot conquer.

Let's look closely at the seven benefits of the shed blood of the Lamb of God. Keep in mind that only a few verses are explored in each section, but there are many more that confirm the truths of each. I strongly encourage you to do some exploring for yourself.

1. Forgiveness. We have been forgiven through the blood of the Lord Jesus Christ. According to Hebrews 9:22, "And almost all things are cleansed with blood, according to the Law, and without the shedding of blood there is no forgiveness." The number one benefit we receive from His shed blood is for our forgiveness. Say this out loud, "I have been forgiven through the blood of Jesus. Thank You, God!"

2. Cleansing. The blood of Jesus cleanses us from all sin. You may wonder, *What's the difference between forgiving and cleansing?* Do you realize that you can be forgiven, but you might still carry a guilty conscience or feel condemned? Cleansing means not only are you forgiven, but also your conscience is cleansed. Let's expand the word *sin* and declare, "The blood of the Lord Jesus Christ has cleansed and cleanses me from all guilt, shame, condemnation, and sin!" First John 1:7 tells us, "But if we walk in the Light as He Himself is in the Light, we have fellowship with one another, and the blood of Jesus His Son cleanses us from all sin." Remember, you are forgiven and cleansed by His blood!

3. Redemption. We have been redeemed by the blood of the Lamb. Ephesians 1:7 says, "In Him we have redemption through His blood, the forgiveness of our wrongdoings, according to the riches of His grace." First Peter 1:18–19 says, "You were not redeemed with perishable things like silver or gold from your futile way of life inherited from your forefathers, but with precious blood, as of a lamb unblemished and spotless, the blood of Christ." The word *redeem* means "to be bought." You were bought and brought out of darkness, transferred out of the domain of darkness into the Kingdom of light (see Colossians 1:13). Remember, you are forgiven, cleansed, and redeemed by His blood!

4. Justification. By the blood of Jesus, you and I are justified. Many believers don't know exactly what justification means, and we can be positionally justified by what Christ has done but not walk in the experiential truth of justification. We are not just forgiven; we are given a brand-new slate. Romans 5:9 (AMP) clearly states, "Therefore, since we have now been justified [declared free of the guilt of sin] by His blood, [how much more certain is it that] we will be saved from the wrath of God through Him." Possibly you've heard to be justified is "just as if I'd" never sinned. This is a clever way to remember the meaning of justification, but let's not forget what happened to that sin. Yes, we have a clean slate, but let us not minimize that all that was on our slate was transferred to Jesus to carry on the cross as 2 Corinthians 5:21 shows us: "For God made Christ, who never sinned, to be the offering for our sin, so that we could be made right with God through Christ." Remember, you are forgiven, cleansed, redeemed, and justified by His blood!

5. Sanctification. Hebrews 10:10 says, "We have been sanctified through the offering of the body of Jesus Christ once for all time." Hebrews 13:12 reveals that "Jesus also suffered outside the gate, that He might sanctify the people through His own blood." You may think, *That sounds nice, but what does that mean to me?*

In 2 Chronicles 5:11 (AMP) we read that "the priests came out of the Holy Place (for all the priests who were present had sanctified themselves [separating themselves from everything unclean]." These priests were set apart from others in Israel to serve God in a very special way. Today, we are "priests" who can approach God on our own through the shed blood of Jesus. We are set apart for good works empowered by the Holy Spirit, which God has planned for us to do (see Ephesians 2:10).

You are not only forgiven, cleansed, redeemed, and justified; you are a set-apart vessel for God's unique purpose. You will be hindered from believing in your destiny until this revelation settles inside you. You have been sanctified by His blood, and because of this you have a destiny, a hope, and a calling.

6. Peace. Through the blood of Jesus we have inner peace. Colossians 1:20 (KJV) reminds us, "And, having made peace through the blood of his cross, by him to reconcile all things unto himself; by him, I say, whether they be things on earth or things in heaven." Jesus made peace through the blood of His cross. So we can declare to our emotions, "Peace, be still." You can speak to the raging storm, "Peace, be still." Remember, you are forgiven, cleansed, redeemed, justified, sanctified, and possess the peace that defies understanding—all by His blood!

7. Access. We have access, confidence, and the freedom to enter into the Most Holy Place through the blood of Jesus. Hebrews 10:19 (AMP) says, "Therefore, believers, since we have confidence and full freedom to enter the Holy Place [the place where God dwells] by [means of] the blood of Jesus." We can also look at Ephesians 2:13–14, which says, "But now in Christ Jesus you who previously were far away have been brought near by the blood of Christ. For He Himself is our peace, who made both groups into one and broke down the barrier of the dividing wall."

To be effective in spiritual warfare, we must know what the blood of the Lamb, Jesus Christ, God's only Son, has accomplished. Then, and only then, have we actualized authority over the prince of the power of the air to disarm evil powers and principalities.

The blood of Jesus is not a good luck charm. The blood of Jesus is powerful—especially when you now learn to apply the blood of the Lamb to your mind, heart, life, family, and in every sphere of responsibility that God has delegated to you.

Darkness stops and life begins when you testify what the blood of Jesus has accomplished. Remember, you are forgiven, cleansed, redeemed, justified, sanctified, peaceful, and have access by His blood!

FOR REFLECTION AND PRAYER

- How does reflecting on how Jesus shed His blood affect how you approach Him through prayer?
- Of the seven benefits of the shed blood of Jesus, which do you feel you know well, and which do you want to access more completely?

- What do you think it means practically to "apply the blood" to your mind, heart, life, family, and in every sphere of responsibility that God has delegated to you?

Take a few moments right now to thank Jesus for His shed blood and to apply the blood to every area of your life.

24

THE SIGNIFICANCE OF
THE LORD'S SUPPER

My friend Lou Engle received a revelation from the Lord that he calls the "Great Communion Revival." He believes that taking the Lord's Supper is one of the important and necessary components leading into another Great Awakening—the great revival that has been prophesied by many and is in the Word of God. Beni Johnson, who has now graduated to be with the Lord, wrote an amazing book on Communion called *The Power of Communion: Accessing Miracles Through the Body and Blood of Jesus*.

Lou Engle had the privilege of meeting with our dear friends, Bill and Beni Johnson of Bethel Church in Redding, California. Lou was directed by a dream from the Lord to go and have Beni lay hands on him. I watched the video in which Lou tells about this very encounter when he asked Beni to lay hands on him so he could help carry on the message of her book, even though he has also been carrying it himself.

I believe it is extremely important for the sacraments and godly traditions of the Church to be restored. This includes the Lord's

Supper. The following are scriptures from the gospel of Matthew and the Corinthian letters of Paul describing the Lord's Supper:

> Now while they were eating, Jesus took some bread, and after a blessing, He broke it and gave it to the disciples, and said, "Take, eat; this is My body." And when He had taken a cup and given thanks, He gave it to them, saying, "Drink from it, all of you; for this is My blood of the covenant, which is being poured out for many for forgiveness of sins. But I say to you, I will not drink of this fruit of the vine from now on until that day when I drink it with you, new, in My Father's kingdom."
>
> Matthew 26:26–29

> Is the cup of blessing which we bless not a sharing in the blood of Christ? Is the bread which we break not a sharing in the body of Christ? Since there is one loaf, we who are many are one body; for we all partake of the one loaf.
>
> 1 Corinthians 10:16–17

> For I received from the Lord that which I also delivered to you, that the Lord Jesus, on the night when He was betrayed, took bread; and when He had given thanks, He broke it and said, "This is My body, which is for you; do this in remembrance of Me." In the same way He also took the cup after supper, saying, "This cup is the new covenant in My blood; do this, as often as you drink it, in remembrance of Me." For as often as you eat this bread and drink the cup, you proclaim the Lord's death until He comes.
>
> Therefore whoever eats the bread or drinks the cup of the Lord in an unworthy way, shall be guilty of the body and the blood of the Lord. But a person must examine himself, and in so doing he is to eat of the bread and drink of the cup.
>
> 1 Corinthians 11:23–28

Jesus and Paul do not say how often to have Communion, but we know the early Church celebrated the Lord's Supper regularly.

Three Major Historical Views of the Lord's Supper

There are different traditions within Christianity regarding the expressions and the meaning of the Lord's Supper. All traditions agree that within the celebration of the Lord's Supper, Eucharist, or Communion, there is the proclamation of the Gospel of the Kingdom that is of primary importance: "Do this in remembrance of Me."

1. A typical Protestant and nondenominational view today is that the bread and the cup (of wine or grape juice) are primarily *symbolic* of the Lord's body and blood. Both outwardly express the inward truth concerning the Lord's passion.

2. The Roman Catholic and some historic Orthodox Church views are termed "transubstantiation," interpreted to mean the bread and the drink are transformed by the miraculous power of God to become the *actual* body and blood of the Lord Jesus Christ.

3. An Anglican, Episcopal, and some other historic liturgical churches hold the view of "consubstantiation," which emphasizes the *real presence* of the Lord as people *participate in* the Eucharist, the Lord's Supper.

Which view have you been taught or do you hold to today? Symbolic, actual, or real presence? I understand the different church views, traditions, and practices of who is qualified to serve the sacraments and I honor the various protocols while holding fast to the revelation of the priesthood of all believers. I personally receive the elements on an almost daily basis and even take them with me wherever I travel. This is a regular part of my devotional walk with God and possibly one of my keys to the anointing.

Regardless of how you see the Communion elements, I pray that the Holy Spirit will highlight the importance of the Lord's Supper and increase your faith as you partake of the bread and the cup.

The Powerful Presence of Jesus in Communion

Let's relook at 1 Corinthians 10:16: "Is the cup of blessing which we bless not a sharing in the blood of Christ? Is the bread which we break not a sharing in the body of Christ?" I believe Paul is saying that there is an authentic blessing that can transpire when receiving the Lord's Supper. This could be referred to as the real presence of the Holy Spirit being released as we enter in by faith in our participation.

I'm concerned that we take the Lord's Supper too lightly. Jonathan Black in his book *The Lord's Supper* tells the true story of Tarcisius, an early Christian martyr for the Lord's Supper. Martyred? For the Lord's Supper? Yes! Read the account with me:

> Tarcisius . . . lived in Rome in the third century where he was part of the Church, possibly a deacon. During a time of fierce persecution (probably under the Emperor Valerian), Tarcisius was given the task of taking Communion to the members of the Church who had been imprisoned for their faith. (In those days, someone would be sent from the church service to take the elements to the sick and imprisoned from the same table around which the whole congregation was gathered for Communion so that the whole church was sharing in the same supper.) On the way from the Communion service to the prison, however, Tarcisius was attacked by a pagan mob who demanded that he hand over the sacrament. But Tarcisius refused. Instead, he clasped it more tightly to protect it with his life. Tarcisius was stoned to death when he wouldn't hand over the Communion.[1]

Tarcisius and the early Church believed that the Lord's Supper is more than mentally remembering and physically swallowing the Communion elements. Taking communion is also an intimate, spiritual act that can transform us physically, mentally, and emotionally. As important as it is to gather and remember, I believe God wants us to expect more. Why? In celebrating the Lord's Supper, we place ourselves between the "already" of the first advent of Christ and the "not yet" of the second advent.

On one occasion a phrase came to me that blessed me deeply: "You have now entered into the understanding of My cup." "The cup" refers to the suffering of Christ. But remember that suffering is not an end in itself. Christ's suffering led to His triumph over sin, sickness, and Satan. Amen! When you take Communion, the real presence of God moves you forward toward victory in Christ.

In an additional time of special worship, the Holy Spirit spoke to me the following: "Communion, the Lord's Supper, is one of the highest and most overlooked weapons of spiritual warfare." I believe this is one of the most significant personal words that the Holy Spirit has ever spoken to me concerning this guide to spiritual warfare.

The Lord's Supper is a powerful weapon for us as we gather in worship, forgive, and receive forgiveness, remember Jesus' broken body and His shed blood, partake of the Communion elements, and experience the tangible presence of God with His empowering grace in our lives. There is a blessing when we fully engage with the presence of Jesus in the Lord's Supper.

Let's do more than only remember. Let's also *encounter* Christ in His Supper. This participation by faith will restore the reverential awe of God and empower our confidence in the precious blood of Jesus, which still speaks loudly when we engage in spiritual warfare. As the classic hymn attests, "There is pow'r, pow'r, wonder-working pow'r in the precious blood of the Lamb!"[2]

FOR REFLECTION AND PRAYER

- The blood of Christ is symbolized and actualized when we partake of Communion, the Lord's Supper. How often do you have Communion at your church? Do you partake at times other than at church?

- What is the significance of Communion for you personally? How special is it to your spiritual life?
- What is your reaction to the Holy Spirit saying, "Communion, the Lord's Supper, is one of the highest and most overlooked weapons of spiritual warfare"?
- Of the three major differences regarding Communion, which one are you most familiar with? How has your view on Communion changed after reading this chapter?

If you are able and have elements for Communion, stop and take the Lord's Supper right now. Acknowledge the real presence of Christ as you celebrate what Jesus has done for you. And the next time you receive Communion with others, hold the elements with the highest respect, knowing what they represent and the One who is present as you eat and drink.

HOW WE OVERCOME BY THE BLOOD

Remember, the lyrics "This is how I fight my battles" from the song "Surrounded (Fight My Battles)"? Well, here is one of the ways I have learned how we overcome. Derek Prince has a prayer proclamation called "By This I Overcome the Devil" that I have prayed for decades:[1]

We overcome Satan when we testify personally to what the Word of God says the blood of Jesus does for us (Revelation 12:11).

Through the blood of Jesus, I am redeemed out of the hand of the devil (Ephesians 1:7).

Through the blood of Jesus, all my sins are forgiven (1 John 1:9).

Through the blood of Jesus, I am continually being cleansed from all sin (1 John 1:7).

Through the blood of Jesus, I am justified, made righteous, just-as-if-I'd never sinned (Romans 5:9).

Through the blood of Jesus, I am sanctified, made holy, set apart to God (Hebrews 13:12).

Through the blood of Jesus, I have boldness to enter into the presence of God (Hebrews 10:19).

The blood of Jesus cries out continually to God in heaven on my behalf (Hebrews 12:24).

How do we overcome? By the blood of the Lamb. Possibly you've heard people pray something like, "I apply the blood over my home," or "I plead the blood over my children." But what does that mean? We combine the blood of the Lamb we receive through the Lord's Supper with the spoken Word of God. Derek Prince's proclamation above is an excellent example of combining scriptural principles, prayerful presentation, and declaration.

Jesus overcame temptation from the devil with "It is written." I will say again that the Kingdom of God is a speech-activated Kingdom. When we combine the finished work of Jesus with His Word, we are empowered to overcome. When the Person of Jesus lives inside of us—the One who bled, died, and now lives—and we combine His real presence with His living Word, the blood speaks.

Where does the phrase "the blood speaks" come from? Let's look at Hebrews 12:22–24 together.

"But you have come to Mount Zion and to the city of the living God, the heavenly Jerusalem, and to myriads of angels, to the general assembly and church of the firstborn who are enrolled in heaven, and to God, the Judge of all, and to the spirits of the righteous made perfect, and to Jesus, the mediator of a new covenant, and to the sprinkled blood, which speaks better than the blood of Abel."

These three insightful verses describe to us a view behind the veil. Here we find, first, a description of God's dwelling place. Second, a picture is painted for us of those who dwell there with God. Last, we are given a presentation of God Himself. In this third phase, we are shown God as the Judge of all, Jesus as our Mediator, and the precious blood that speaks.

Does blood speak? We find the answer to that question in Genesis 4:10, which records what God said to Cain after he killed his brother Abel: "The voice of your brother's blood is crying out to Me from the ground." What was Abel's blood saying? Abel's innocent blood was crying out for vengeance.

The Lord heard the blood of Abel that had been poured out onto the ground and came to the scene. Perhaps Abel's blood was shouting, "Vengeance! I want vengeance!" But before the presence of our Judge in heaven, there is a "blood which speaks better than the blood of Abel." What does this blood declare? The innocent blood of Jesus is a continuous reminder before our Father of the sacrifice of His Son who took upon Himself the wrath of God against all injustice.

The blood of Abel spoke out for vengeance, but the blood of Jesus speaks out, "Mercy, mercy, mercy be!" This is how we fight our battles—this is how we overcome! Remember, God's Kingdom is a speech-activated Kingdom! We don't let go! Along with Jesus, we declare, "It is finished!"

Highly influential pastor Charles Spurgeon said, "The blood of Jesus . . . unlocks the treasury of heaven. Many keys fit many locks, but the master-key is the blood and the name of Him that died but rose again, and ever lives in heaven to save unto the uttermost."[2]

Tools to Overcome

So how can we take all we've learned and put it to practical use in spiritual warfare? Here are some examples:

- When you get a bad health report or a part of your body is not functioning well, apply the blood and declare over what is not well, "Jesus, you are the One who heals me" (see Exodus 15:26).
- When you experience a financial loss or are gripped by the fear of lack, plead the blood over your finances and call out to your Provider, thanking Him for supplying all your

needs according to His riches in Christ Jesus (see Philippians 4:19).

- When you get into a fight with your spouse, stop the argument, plead the blood over your marriage, and declare, "God has joined us together, and nothing will separate us" (see Mark 10:9).

- When you are stressed, apply the blood to your mind and declare to your storm, "Peace, be still. Jesus is keeping me in perfect peace because my mind is steadfast and I will trust in You" (see Isaiah 26:3).

You may want to start a proclamation prayer journal in this format. Put the name of what you are battling at the top of the page. Then write your proclamations with specific scriptures to fight that battle. There are also wonderful Bible promises books you can reference. In addition to God's warfare armor given to us in Ephesians 6, remember that you can always enforce the victory over the powers of darkness by pleading the blood repeatedly and agreeing with Christ's triumphant cry, "It is finished!"

──────── **FOR REFLECTION AND PRAYER** ────────

- What unjust situation do you see that needs you to cry out in prayer, "Mercy! Lord Jesus, have mercy!"?
- What area in your life do you want the name of Jesus, the blood of Jesus, and the power of the Holy Spirit to confront?

Take a few moments right now to plead the blood of Jesus over situations in your life that need His intervention and leadership.

VICTORIOUS SPIRITUAL WARFARE PRAYER

Glory to God in the highest! There is wonder-working power in the blood of the Lamb, and nothing but the blood of Jesus can wash away my sins!

Thank You for shedding Your innocent blood so humbly and generously for me. I declare that not one drop will be wasted. By His blood, I am forgiven, cleansed, and redeemed. Because of the blood of Jesus, You see me as if I have never sinned. You have set me apart into a holy calling for the Almighty God. I not only have peace through the cross, but I also have access into Your most holy throne room. I call forth the blood of Jesus and apply it to the doorpost of my mind, my heart, my hands, and every member of my body to bring all of me into obedience to You.

I claim Psalm 107:2 (AMP) for myself, "Let the redeemed of the LORD say so, whom He has redeemed from the hand of the adversary." I say so! You provided the blood of Jesus that speaks love, rather than the blood of Abel that cries out for vengeance. I have the blood from my Brother Christ Jesus that cries out, "Mercy, mercy, mercy be!" And in response I say, "Yes and amen! Let mercy rule over judgment!" Amen.

DEALING WITH TERRITORIAL SPIRITS

But if it is by the Spirit of God that I cast out the demons, then the kingdom of God has come upon you [before you expected it]. Or how can anyone go into a strong man's house and steal his property unless he first overpowers and ties up the strong man? Then he will ransack and rob his house.

Matthew 12:28–29 AMP

Some believers consider the topic of territorial spirits both a complex and controversial subject. I consider insight on the territoriality among the demonic host absolutely necessary, even a vital aspect of our victorious spiritual warfare.

231

I'm grateful to all of the forerunners I quote in this section who not only know about this subject theoretically, but also have dealt with territorial spirits experientially. Together, let's learn more about these tiered demonic spirits of darkness that attempt to infiltrate and even govern over geographic regions or spheres of influence.

Yes, we have Good News! In previous chapters, we have been exposed to the truth of the power that is in the name of Jesus. We have also learned about the authority that occurs when we testify what the blood of Jesus has already accomplished. Remember, there is power in the blood of the Lamb!

26

THE TERRITORIALITY OF THE DEMONIC HOST

The storm on the Sea of Galilee as told in Mark 4:35–41 is a clear picture of territorial demons. Let's look at what happened step by step, how both Jesus and His disciples responded, and what we can learn to help us in our own battles with territorial spirits.

After a long day of teaching, Jesus tells His disciples that He wants to cross over to the other side of the sea. Along the way Jesus falls asleep on a cushion in the stern of the ship. A storm comes up and the wind and waves get way out of control—even for experienced fishermen.

We can see here that the men are trying to go from one point to the next; they're in a place of transition and the storm is hindering them from reaching next divine appointment. The storm is attempting to prevent a major miracle that was waiting for them on the other side of the sea. Jesus had said, "Let's go over to the other side" (verse 35). Often when you make a decision or declaration to move progressively forward with the Lord, there will be a counterattack by the enemy to hinder you from going to the next level.

What was the force behind this storm? Was this just a coincidental storm or a demonic entity trying to hinder the divine appointment waiting for Jesus and His disciples? We can answer this question if we know what Jesus was addressing when He said, "Quiet! Be still!" (verse 39 NIV). I believe Jesus was addressing simultaneously the realm of the known, seeable, natural plane of life and the parallel realm of the supernatural, which operates in the unseen realm behind the scenes.

After the disciples wake up Jesus, He does three actions:

1. He gets up.
2. He rebukes the wind. Various Bible translations use the words, "Peace!" "Hush!" "Silence!" and "Calm down!"
3. He releases a declaration in the opposite spirit of the chaotic storm: "Peace, be still."

Note that Jesus has to be awakened from sleep by the disciples. Jesus is not fretting wondering if the boat will be overcome by the waves. But the disciples are afraid because they are in the wrong dimension. In the same way that the disciples go to Jesus in the storm, so must we.

After Jesus gets up, He rebukes the wind. The word *wind* here can also be a similar word, or the same word, for *spirit*. Jesus rebukes the wind, and then He releases the declaration. The declaration does not come first—the rebuke does. This is important. Why? Because there is a spiritual force operating behind the storm.

The result is that the disciples' fear of the circumstances turns into the fear of the Lord. Verse 41 (NLT) reads, "The disciples were absolutely terrified. 'Who is this man?' they asked each other. 'Even the wind and waves obey him!'"

The next chapter of Mark details the divine appointment the storm was seeking to disrupt. On the other side of the sea was a man full of demons, and those demons did not want to leave their geographical sphere or allotted territory of jurisdiction. Mark

5:9–10 (NIV) continues the story: "Then Jesus asked him, 'What is your name?' 'My name is Legion,' he replied, 'for we are many.' And he begged Jesus again and again not to send them out of the area."

Why didn't the demons in the region of the Gerasenes not want to leave? Perhaps they were assigned by Satan to rule in that particular geographical sphere or region. We know the demonic forces did not want to leave or be assigned elsewhere.

The World's Boundaries Are Set by God

Have you thought about how the boundaries of nations, territories, regions, and the like are all set by God? Deuteronomy 32:8 (NLT) says, "When the Most High assigned lands to the nations, when he divided up the human race, he established the boundaries of the peoples according to the number in his heavenly court."

Also consider Acts 17:26: "He made from one man every nation of mankind to live on all the face of the earth, having determined their *appointed times* and the *boundaries* of their habitation" (emphasis added). God sets boundaries in place for all nations, and we are to call forth the redemptive purpose and prophetic destiny of our nation, province, state, city, and community.

We must also look at 2 Chronicles 7:14: "[If] My people who are called by My name humble themselves, pray and seek My face, and turn from their wicked ways, then I will hear from heaven, and I will forgive their sin and will heal their land." Note that God is focused not only on people, but also *land*. Just as there are distinct destinies and purposes set for people or a specific geographical region, so there is a distinct, counter plot of the enemy to try to undermine and destroy the purposes of God for people groups and geographical regions.

Satan desires to possess regions and fill them with his evil spirits, plans, and influences. According to Revelation 2:13, Satan has a place from which he governs his evil forces. It says, "I know where you dwell, where Satan's throne is; . . . where Satan dwells." Satan has specific dwelling places within certain cities, which are considered specific strongholds of evil.

Strategic Lessons from the Life of Daniel

A throne is a place from which a ruler exercises dominion. The entity, whether good or evil, releases its influence from that throne over that specific region or place. We can gain a lot of insight from the life of Daniel, and one of the lessons to consider is on the theme of a spiritual prince being over certain geopolitical realms.

Daniel 10 records an intriguing encounter. After Daniel had received a revelation of a significant future war, he fasted and prayed for three weeks. An angel appeared to him in response. No one saw the angel except Daniel, yet those with him fled in terror. More than likely, they felt its presence, though they did not see the angel. While gazing at the vision, Daniel lost all his physical strength and fell into a trance, a deep sleep. The supernatural being identified himself as an angel of God and told Daniel that as a result of Daniel's prayers, a great struggle took place between Michael, the archangel of God, and an evil, supernatural prince of the ancient kingdom of Persia.

The "one who looked like a man" (verse 18 NIV) then touched Daniel and gave him supernatural strength. He told Daniel, "Do not be afraid, you who are highly esteemed, Peace! Be strong now; be strong." Then he left Daniel and returned to assist in the spiritual midheaven war against the prince of Persia.

What happened in response to Daniel's humility and prayer? God sent an angel directly to Daniel. But his arrival was delayed because the "prince of Persia" temporarily hindered the angel for twenty-one days. This clearly is not a human prince; it is an "exalted being" able to resist so much that the archangel Michael had to be summoned for help.

"The prince of the kingdom of Persia," the biblical phrase from verse 13, was a demonic being assigned by Satan to this nation, special area, or geopolitical sphere of activity. He was to hinder God's will or Kingdom there, especially among God's people under Persian rule. That doesn't mean that the Persian people were evil.

The prince of Greece is also mentioned (see verse 20). Perhaps there is at least one high-ranking demonic power assigned to each nation, with lesser demonic entities to assist. Evidently these demonic forces were engaged in warfare with the angelic host of heaven, the prize being the opportunity to manipulate earthly nations and peoples. Michael, a warrior archangel, is portrayed as the special guardian over Israel (see Daniel 12:1).

Three Implications from Daniel's Vision

There are at least three important lessons we can glean from Daniel 10 that are pertinent for us in our effective spiritual warfare lessons today.

First, Daniel's prayer provoked a heavenly battle, which he was not fully aware of until the angel appeared and told him.

Second, according to Daniel 10:12 Daniel's prayers were also used to release angelic reinforcements. Daniel 12:18 supports evidence that a new level of strength was released to him by the angelic army warring for the purposes of God. Does this suggest that the outcome of the heavenly conflict is dependent on the frequency or the fervency of your and my prayers? I personally believe so, both from a biblical and personal testimonial level. I have written at length about this subject in my book *Angelic Encounters Today* in the chapter "Angelic Intervention through Intercession."

Third, the battles on earth and their outcomes reflect the involvement of heaven. In other words, there is more to historical conflict than we can humanly see. We can also look at 2 Kings 6:15–17 (NIV) regarding spiritual battles beyond what we can see:

> When the servant of the man of God got up and went out early the next morning, an army with horses and chariots had surrounded

the city. "Oh no, my lord! What shall we do?" the servant asked. "Don't be afraid," the prophet answered. "Those who are with us are more than those who are with them." And Elisha prayed, "Open his eyes, LORD, so that he may see." Then the LORD opened the servant's eyes, and he looked and saw the hills full of horses and chariots of fire all around Elisha.[1]

It is important to understand that we deal with different hierarchical layers of darkness controlled by the enemy so we can fight effectively. Territorial spirits are in a sense "regional managers" that oversee larger spheres of influence beyond what a singular demonic spirit that is designed to afflict a human being oversees. We must learn to identify their legal basis to rule, remove it through repentance and confession of sin, and then engage in authoritative intercession. (Many of my resources build upon one another. They become complimentary building materials when brought together, such as with *Deliverance from Darkness*, *Strike the Mark*, *The Lifestyle of a Watchman*, and *Praying with God's Heart*.)

Yes, we all battle against evil, and Christ has given us all we need to win that battle. In the next chapter we'll see how we can use the additional tools of spiritual mapping and prophetic insight to discern properly so we can fight wisely and triumph.

───── **FOR REFLECTION AND PRAYER** ─────

- When have you encountered a "storm" before a divine assignment?
- God sets boundaries for all nations, and you are called to participate in the redemptive purpose and the prophetic destiny of your nation, province, state, city, and community. How are you engaged in that assignment?

- When have you sensed that your prayers are provoking a heavenly battle? What have you seen with your spiritual eyes?

Take a few moments right now to talk to God about where He wants you to have spiritual influence and how He wants you to govern what He has entrusted to you.

27

SPIRITUAL MAPPING

The goal of spiritual mapping is to discover the doors through which Satan and his demonic host gain access into and influence over a family, geographic area, city, a cultural sphere of influence, or even a nation. We identify the demonic attack, target our prayers effectively, and strategize to shut these portals.

Spiritual mapping can reveal the moral or legal grounds on which a stronghold is built in that location, as well as the demonic spirits that energize it. When dealing with territorial spirits, spiritual mapping is a helpful tool in discerning and praying effectively. Then we can act appropriately with our informed team-based approach to spiritual warfare.

Below are some helpful insights about spiritual mapping from respected Christian leaders who taught on and led strategic intercessory and spiritual mapping initiatives.

Spiritual mapping is an attempt to look beyond and behind the natural, material, and physical features of a city to the spiritual forces that give it shape and influence its character. It involves superimposing our understanding of forces and events in the spiritual domain onto places and circumstances in the material world. If we are to understand why things are the way they are today, we must first examine what happened yesterday. We must solve the riddle of the origin of territorial strongholds.[1]

George Otis Jr.

Spiritual mapping gives us an image or spiritual photograph of the situation in the heavenly places above us. What an X ray is to a physician, spiritual mapping is to intercessors. It is a supernatural vision that shows us the enemy's blinds, location, number, weapons, and above all, how the enemy can be defeated.[2]

Harold Caballeros

Spiritual mapping is an attempt to see the world around us as it really is, not as it appears to be. . . . It reveals the invisible powers, both good and evil, behind visible features of everyday life. In mapping a community, the first step is to gather the information, and the second step is to act on the information. The prayer action will be more effective if it is based on a solid foundation.[3]

C. Peter Wagner

A stronghold is a fortified place that Satan builds to exalt himself against the knowledge and plans of God. . . . [Satan] cleverly cloaks strongholds under the guise often of culture.[4]

Cindy Jacobs

We can pray in the Spirit and get information from the Holy Spirit, but we must also pray with our understanding. The basic concept of spiritual mapping is that we need to be as well-informed as possible when we are praying.[5]

Kjell Sjöberg

I love the heart behind this last quote, which highlights the goal of spiritual mapping: "to be as well-informed as possible" in our spiritual warfare.

Strategic Level Spiritual Warfare

There are six principles for spiritual warfare I believe are necessary for us to keep in mind as we gaze deeper into our assignments from the Lord and pray onsite with spiritual insight.

1. Our ministry must be based on God's Word.
2. We must be living in a place of purity and holiness before we engage in overt engagement.
3. We must be sent by God in His proper time and with His authority.
4. We must conduct our research according to the instructions we have received from those we are walking in alignment with.
5. We must then report our instructions and/or information and/or revelation without personal or prejudicial opinions or bias. This is extraordinarily important.
6. We must keep our attitude of faith in the Word and power of God.

Kjell Sjöberg, one of the spiritual warfare pioneers from the past, encourages us by saying, "Individuals exist today with the gift for prophetic espionage. Certain people who have experience of God's holiness and of His steadfast love, while in worship before Him, have been given a haunting instinct to track down the enemy's manipulations. They do this then by targeted prayer that follows detailed spiritual mapping."[6]

The Church is called to do more than simply stand firm and defend. When Jesus spoke of the Church, He said "the gates of hell will not prevail against it" (Matthew 16:18 KJV). In other words, as the Church moves forward, the very gates of hell cannot stop us. The Church is required to actively seek out, uncover, and thus confront the demonic power that influences our corporate existence. With this knowledge, spiritual leaders and their discerning intercessors are better equipped to pray and work together toward the dismantling of the strongholds over a region. After finding these strongholds, they may pursue strategic, wisdom-filled courses of action to open up opportunities for evangelization of the lost and the discipling of spheres of culture.

A fundamental theological assumption of spiritual mapping and strategic-level spiritual warfare is that Satan's schemes extend beyond individuals and churches to entire cities, regions, cultural spheres of society, and even nations. In other words, spiritual mapping provides a spiritual blueprint or X-ray revealing the territorial spirits that are temporarily ruling in the midheavens over a geopolitical sphere or territory.

As gifted disciples in Christ Jesus, we are called to expose and nullify their schemes and deceitful purposes, and then displace them by declaring God's prophetic destiny.

A Clear Word from the Lord

Some years ago when I was ministering in New York City, the voice of the Lord clearly came to me one morning. I had already been a student of spiritual warfare for many years, and I was avidly researching the different views on territorial spirits.

Finally, this word from the Holy Spirit was clearly spoken to me and became very helpful: "I am about to release new levels of identification and intercession whereby the legal basis of the rights of the powers of the air to remain will be removed." That one sentence solved a lot of puzzles and questions for me, and I believe after all these years, I'm still gaining insight into that word the Holy Spirit audibly spoke to me that morning.

Revelation, interpretation, and application is an essential age-old threefold process of discerning and implementing information from the Holy Spirit. *Revelation* must be followed by proper *interpretation*, and then by strategic *application* for spiritual mapping and for anything that deals with the prophetic. If you get it wrong on the first or second step, you will certainly have it wrong on the important third step of application; but we can learn from the errors of the past. Right? And let's make sure that we do on this important subject so that we will grow in maturity in spiritual warfare.

Some people are throwing out today what they had in other movements because there was damaging excess or abuse. But let's hold on to the good and learn from the errors of the past. Let's walk in humility, seek the Lord, receive confirmation, walk with others, and then move out in confidence with the blueprints and strategies that the Holy Spirit confirms and supplies, to identify and disarm powers and principalities in Jesus' name.

FOR REFLECTION AND PRAYER

- Why are the six principles for spiritual mapping so essential?
- How does the goal of spiritual mapping—to be as informed as possible so we can engage in spiritual warfare most effectively—affect you personally?
- When has spiritual insight into a region, city, or place helped you to pray more effectively? How did you engage in spiritual warfare differently?

Take a few moments right now to ask God how He may want you to gain additional insight through mapping the spiritual roots of where you live.

28

How to Wisely Confront Powers of Darkness

Have you ever seen a demon manifest through a person and attempted to participate in casting it out? It can be quite exhilarating and quite a learning curve at the same time. While deliverance ministry seems to be increasing in the Body of Christ today, most believers still have little experience in the casting out of evil spirits. I also don't want to see the continuation of presumptuous approaches that confront spiritual powers too casually with overfamiliarity. Jude warned of people who "scoff at supernatural beings" (NIV) because even "Michael the archangel, when he disputed with the devil and argued about the body of Moses, did not dare pronounce against him an abusive judgment, but said, 'The Lord rebuke you!'" (Jude 9 NASB).

I have been involved in various levels and applications of spiritual warfare for years. We must avoid both ditches of excess that can get us off track. On one side is neutered passivity, which says it is unwise or illegal to directly confront the powers of darkness. The other side is the ditch of excessive confrontation, which rebukes demonic entities before removing the legal basis of their right to temporarily reign.

Over the years, I have seen many approaches and been blessed to observe a healthier integrated model emerge. C. Peter Wagner, in his book on spiritual warfare,[1] did much research and networking, and then he presented the following three levels of confronting these powers:

1. **Ground-level spiritual warfare.** This involves breaking off demonic hindrances and casting demons out of people. Please read my book *Deliverance from Darkness* for detailed teaching on this subject.

2. **Occult-level spiritual warfare.** This level of spiritual warfare deals with demonic forces released through activities related to Satanism, witchcraft, Freemasonry, Eastern religions, New Age, shamanism, astrology, and many other forms of structured occultism. Wicca is one of the fastest-growing recognized religions filling the void of a powerless traditional Church. This trend must change. We must have a Holy Spirit–saturated people who move in signs and wonders and are not confined inside the four walls of a church building. We are the *Ekklesia*, the called-out ones, who carry the authority of the name of Jesus everywhere we go.

3. **Strategic-level spiritual warfare.** Confrontation with high-ranking principalities and powers, such as Paul wrote about in Ephesians 6:12, requires strategic-level spiritual warfare and battle plans. These enemy forces are frequently called territorial spirits because they attempt to infiltrate and network through neighborhoods, regions, cities, nations, people groups, and religious allegiances to undermine Christian values and traditions. Some businesses are actually cults today; and some forms of societies, secret associations, and underground cultures keep people in spiritual captivity.

Proper Confrontation

To properly and wisely confront these powers, I recommend four guidelines:

1. We must hear the Lord. Jesus was very clear that His sheep (His followers) hear His voice (see John 10:27). We must learn to listen to the Holy Spirit before we engage in battle—great or small. We are all called to hear from God and respond in some way to His voice. Partnering with seasoned Christian leaders—specifically apostles and prophets—becomes key in taking and maintaining territory. It is not enough to just temporarily displace evil; we must maintain the purity of the place we have attained and claimed for God's Kingdom. My book and materials on *Hearing God's Voice Today* provide practical, proven approaches that have helped many people.

2. We must remit corporate sins, moving in identificational repentance. We are all called to repent of our own sins. Other times we are given the opportunity to confess the sins of others we identify with. For example, I, as a man, can identify with the sins of other men and repent of those sins corporately, which can bring a breakthrough in the spirit.

At times I refer to this as "ambassadorial intercession." Insights about identification repentance allow us to get to the root of key issues. Now is the time to go for the root systems in present-day society—to heal spiritual sicknesses, dealing with causes rather than symptoms only. My book *Strike the Mark* is a helpful resource in this area of spiritual warfare.

3. The Church must engage the enemy in strategic-level spiritual warfare. Principles of strategic-level spiritual warfare need to be employed to clear the way so that God's Kingdom can be advanced in heaven as it is on earth.

Please understand that believers are called to different levels. Some are called to level 1 (ground level), others to level 2 (occult level), and some to level 3 (strategic level)—but we are all called to participate together in advancing God's Kingdom and taking ground for Him. We all need to be engaged. Remember, as I state in my Global Prayer Storm class, "Every prayer counts and every sacrifice matters."

4. We must not spew abusive language at the devil. We are never called to move in an accusatory manner against the powers of darkness or bring a judgment of blasphemy. It is flat-out not scriptural. I mentioned Jude 9 earlier, which states that even the archangel Michael "did not dare bring an abusive condemnation against [Satan]" (AMP).

The name of Jesus is never to be used in vain. We need to learn how to remove the legal basis by which Satan can resist believers and/or people in an area and not indulge in immature approaches and inappropriate applications. We are each called to be ambassadors of Christ.

Releasing the Seven Spirits into the Seven Spheres of Society

In 1975 two Christian leaders—Loren Cunningham, founder of Youth with a Mission, and Bill Bright, founder of Campus Crusade for Christ (now called Cru in the U.S.)—were praying separately about how to turn their nation back to Jesus. God gave each man seven areas of society to concentrate on, and when they met together, they discovered their lists contained the same areas.

Today these areas are often called the seven cultural mountains. These seven spheres of society can be described with the following words:

1. Family
2. Government (politics)
3. Education
4. Economy
5. Religion (spirituality)

6. Arts (entertainment, sports)

7. Media (communication)

Demonic forces of darkness are intent on invading and capturing not only people, but also regions, cities, nations, people groups, religious allegiances, businesses, industries, and every form of society and culture with the goal of keeping people in spiritual captivity.

Expanding upon this evil strategy, the powers of darkness attempt to set up thrones of iniquity in or through these seven spheres of society. Specific demonic spirits, such as Leviathan, Jezebel, witchcraft, and others, specifically target each sphere of influence, attempting to infiltrate the leadership with corruption and every evil thing.

But God has had a plan from the very beginning.

Into each of these seven spheres of human society and civilization come the seven Spirits of God: "The Spirit of the Lord . . . the spirit of wisdom and understanding, the spirit of counsel and strength, the spirit of knowledge and the fear of the LORD" (Isaiah 11:2). How do these seven Spirits of God work on earth? Through God's messengers, His faithful ones—you and me—and through His angels. Revelation 5:6 (AMP, emphasis added) declares:

> And there between the throne (with the four living creatures) and among the elders I saw a Lamb (Christ) standing, [bearing scars and wounds] as though it had been slain, with seven horns (complete power) and with seven eyes (complete knowledge), which are the *seven Spirits of God* who have been sent [on duty] into all the earth.

Today, the Holy Spirit in all His fullness is sending forth into the entire world believers who are filled with His Spirit, who carry His impact and influence everywhere they go. When Jesus dispatched His disciples, did He say, "Go, therefore, and make disciples of some parts of the nations"? No! Jesus said, "Go, therefore, and make disciples of all the nations," carrying the Light of the world into the world (Matthew 28:19).

To each of these seven cultural spheres of society, God is raising up discerning, praying believers to move in the opposite spirit of the powers of darkness. This army of God releases the seven identifiable expressions of the Holy Spirit to displace the demonic host, raise up godly influencers, and enthrone the One who is worthy.

Ten Points of Agreement for the Battle

Those who seek to confront the dark forces of the enemy in the midheavens have different views and approaches. Some question if we have the right and authority to directly address principalities, territorial spirits, and the like, and if there is a direct biblical model to do so. The apostolic epistles include twenty-four written prayers that all address the Father in the name of Jesus for the release of the Spirit, but none of these portray what is considered a specific, confrontive assault against the powers of darkness. Let's not confuse the issues of personal deliverance ministry with strategic-level spiritual warfare.

Most all agree that we are to directly address evil spirits in the personal deliverance ministry of individuals. Where people disagree is how to address principalities and powers.

Some believe we have authority in the horizontal plane or earthly sphere, but not in the vertical plane or second heaven dimension. This view promotes that we should petition the Father and let Him address these forces in the midheavens as He chooses. But if a principality manifests in your earthly sphere, then we can address it because it stepped out of the heavenlies to enter our sphere of authority.

Others state that God has "seated us with Him in the heavenly places in Christ Jesus" (Ephesians 2:6) so we do have authority for both the vertical and the horizontal planes of spiritual warfare. This raises the question, "What made that prince step out of its domain into yours?" When you logically and spiritually attempt to fully understand this reasoning, it is easy to find that it leads to as many questions as it does answers, though the intent is sincere.

I think a good question for us to ask is, "Must we always have a clearly laid-out biblical model to be led by the Spirit in spiritual warfare tactics? If the directive is unclear in Scripture, is it therefore illegal?" I believe that God has the right to bring forth applications for a particular people, time, and situation that are not fully detailed in Scripture. We can trust the Holy Spirit to lead us as we choose to follow the guidelines of His Word with the weapons He has given to us.

Luke 10:19 says clearly, "I have given you authority over all the power of the enemy." He gave His disciples power and authority over *all* the power of the enemy. How much is all? All the power of the enemy must include principalities and spirits of wickedness in the heavenly places. So the issue is *how* this is accomplished, not *if*.

Even though the Church may disagree about the application of what territorial spiritual warfare looks like when fighting these powers of darkness, there are ten principles I believe we all can agree upon:

1. There is a spiritual battle that continues.
2. God wants us to continue to intercede and petition the Father for the release of the power and gifting of the Holy Spirit.
3. We must rid ourselves of prideful self-promotion because we each can fall prey to the same attitude that caused Lucifer to fall.
4. Every believer in Christ Jesus has authority to set captives free from demonic torment.
5. Strongholds of the mind are to be resisted and brought captive to Christ's Kingdom life.

6. We are all commissioned to do the works of Christ of feeding the poor, healing the sick, evangelizing the lost, setting the captives free, and proclaiming the Good News.

7. Our goal is to be Christ centered, not devil conscious, and to win for the Lamb the reward of His suffering.

8. Power and authority over the enemy is delegated to us through the triumph of the cross of Christ.

9. This battle, ultimately, is not ours but the Lord's!

10. We are called to be Kingdom enforcers of what Christ Jesus has already accomplished on the cross of Calvary because "It is finished!"

Five Keys to Kingdom Advancement for Every Sphere

An underlying truth for strategic spiritual warfare against territorial spirits is that you must remain under divine authority to bring Kingdom advancement on earth. God has given you a sphere of influence and authority, and it's important to know what that sphere is.

What is your sphere of authority? What authority do you have in your family, neighborhood, church, ministry, city? Your sphere may grow over time, so your authority is ever-changing. Where you have the greatest authority is where you will have the greatest success in spiritual warfare.

The following are five essential keys for Kingdom advancement for every sphere of life, ministry, and society:

1. *Abiding.* We cultivate an intimate relationship with God. Seek the Lord and pursue a relationship with Him.

2. *Appropriation.* We receive divine authority. God has given all you need for your Kingdom assignment.

3. *Action.* We must step out in faith. Start praying where God has planted you and be faithful to obey what you hear.

4. *Anointing.* Our efforts are empowered by the Holy Spirit. The Anointed One is with you and it is His power that saves, not your human efforts.

5. *Advancement.* We see the Lord's Kingdom gain ground. Make a difference in the sphere He's entrusted to you.

Please hear me out. There is no specific special spiritual gift in the Bible called spiritual warfare. We all can implement these foundational keys to triumph in spiritual warfare. Every believer is called to discern, praise, worship, and intercede in prayer. This is the birthright of every believer, and God invites you to do your part.

FOR REFLECTION AND PRAYER

- Of the three levels of strategic warfare, which one do you think has the most devastating effect on the Church? On your personal life?
- Of the four proper and wise ways to confront evil powers, which one would be the most effective way for you?
- What is the difference between the issues of deliverance ministry and strategic spiritual warfare?
- To what degree are you engaged using the five essential keys for Kingdom advancement?

Take a few moments right now to talk to God about your desire to draw closer to Him with intimate fellowship.

VICTORIOUS SPIRITUAL WARFARE PRAYER

Father God, You are awesome! You have seated me in heavenly places alongside Your Son, Jesus, who is majestically enthroned far above all powers and principalities and spirits of wickedness, even those in the midheavens. I do not simply pray from earth up through the powers of darkness; rather, I ascend through worship and praise, and I enter Your very throne room.

I pray with the heart of Jesus and declare that Your objective on earth to reap a great harvest of souls is also my objective. I desire to win for the Lamb the reward of His sufferings. I am called by You to identify and map out the spiritual hindrances that stand in the way of Your plans and purposes and remove them, in Jesus' great name.

I welcome heaven's army of angels and the fullness of the seven Spirits of God to be released into the earth realm today. Dear God, release Your Kingdom advancement power in me to influence my sphere of life and ministry in society together with other believers. Thank You for leading me in victorious spiritual warfare for Your glory. Amen and amen.

ENFORCING CALVARY'S VICTORY

And they overcame him [Satan] because of the blood of the Lamb and because of the word of their testimony, and they did not love their life even when faced with death.

Revelation 12:11

What a privilege we have to partner with the Holy Spirit to enforce the victory Jesus gained for us at Calvary! This is what this last section is all about. But let's first summarize where we've been.

God created heaven and earth without a flaw. God also created Lucifer, an anointed covering cherub, and assigned him with the special task of worship in the heavens. He, however, became proud of his own wisdom and beauty and aspired to a position equal with God. Lucifer systematically promoted rebellion and seduced one third of the angels to break their loyalty to God and assault God's throne. For this, Lucifer and the angels under his charge were cast down from the highest heaven—the heaven of God's dwelling place.

Then these created beings set up a competing kingdom. Jesus said that he saw Lucifer fall into the earth realm like lightning from the heavens above. The saga continued as Genesis 3 records the temptation of Adam and Eve, the first man and woman, by Lucifer, the crafty serpent, which led to their fall, judgment by God, and banishment from the Garden of Eden.

The greatest war of all began, and all humankind has since been born into that struggle. There is no neutral ground or middle position for anyone. We are either on one side of this great cosmic battle or the other. As I have said repeatedly throughout this book, we are born *in* war, and we are born *for* war. Now press pause and repeat that statement out loud! "I was born *in* war, and I was born *for* war!"

So where are we today? Satan's objective is to steal, kill, and destroy—to keep those who do not yet know God blinded from the truth, and to hinder followers of Jesus from entering the full purposes of God on the earth so that He is glorified and worshiped. Satan desires to gain as much control as possible of the world's systems and to receive universal worship for himself.

The Father desires than none should perish but all come to know and love His Son, Jesus, who said as He was leaving earth, "All authority in heaven and on earth has been given to Me. Go, therefore." (Matthew 28:18–19). This same authority He has entrusted to His children to wage war with Satan and his forces, wrestling with them using powerful spiritual weapons, enforcing Calvary's victory so that we see the greatest harvest of souls history has ever known before the return Jesus.

In the final chapters of this book, we take a fresh look at where our triumph is rooted—the finished work of the cross. We close out this comprehensive guide by courageously moving out in faith, crushing darkness under our feet, to advance the Kingdom of God for the glory of Jesus.

29

THE WORK OF THE CROSS AND PRINCIPLES OF BATTLE

Have you ever wondered what was going through Satan's mind as Jesus walked the earth? He had heard God declare that a Descendant of Eve would crush his head (see Genesis 3:15), so Satan was surely watching for any way to stop the Messiah from being born. After Jesus escaped Herod's evil plot to kill all the babies Jesus' age and then soundly defeated Satan's temptations in the wilderness, Satan continued to look for opportune times to cause Him to fall (see Luke 4:13).

One of those times came just before Jesus went to the cross, and the temptation came through one of Jesus' most passionate followers: Peter. Lucifer's base had been established through pride, rebellion, disobedience, deceit, darkness, and destruction. Now he was contending with the King of Glory walking as a Man, humble in submission to the Father and in every point obedient, shining brightly as the Light of the world.

Although Jesus cast out demons throughout His ministry, releasing individuals from Satan and his legions, that deliverance was only a foretaste of Jesus' plan to destroy the very base of satanic rule. What would be the tool to destroy the works of the enemy? The work of the cross.

Jesus spoke of impending death to His disciples to prepare them for what was ahead. But what Peter specifically was not prepared for was to be a voice for Satan. Read the account from Matthew 16:21–23 (NIV):

> From that time on Jesus began to explain to his disciples that he must go to Jerusalem and suffer many things at the hands of the elders, the chief priests and the teachers of the law, and that he must be killed and on the third day be raised to life.
>
> Peter took him aside and began to rebuke him. "Never, Lord!" he said. "This shall never happen to you!"
>
> Jesus turned and said to Peter, "Get behind me, Satan! You are a stumbling block to me; you do not have in mind the concerns of God, but merely human concerns."

Jesus was headed toward the cross and Satan was attempting to disrupt His mission. Just days before His death, Jesus explained exactly what was going to happen: "Now judgment is upon this world. Now the ruler of this world will be cast out. And if I am lifted up from the earth, I will draw all people to Myself." Jesus was ramping up for the punch that would knock out the enemy!

To His disciples at the Last Supper Jesus revealed, "I will no longer talk much with you, for the ruler of this world is coming, and he has nothing in Me" (NKJV). I love the phrase "he has nothing in Me." Satan had nothing that could entangle the perfect Lamb of God who voluntarily yielded to the hands of sinful men inspired by Satan and his demons to bring suffering and mockery to the holy Son of God. What the prince of darkness and his host failed to discern was that for every drop of blood they caused to flow from the Savior's veins, untold scores would be released from the domination of this proud, twisted creature.

The work of the cross, this altar of sacrifice, destroyed the works of the devil—sin and sickness, suffering and torment, rejection and shame. The Son of Man took all poverty and abandonment upon Himself on that tree. Human seed, previously bound, would now be freed to receive by faith all that belonged to the eternal Son of God.

When Jesus cried out on Calvary's cross, "It is finished," and surrendered His spirit, He did more than die for the sins of the world. He declared the end of the old regime ruled by Satan. Heaven's veil was torn in two. God and man could again enjoy sweet fellowship. When Jesus rose from the dead, darkness lost and life prevailed.

In appearing to His disciples after His resurrection, Jesus said, "All power and authority is given to Me in heaven and in earth" (Matthew 28:18). The Worthy One regained the earth from the prince of the world system. Then Jesus sent His followers into the world as ambassadors of heaven to proclaim and reveal His Lordship. Jesus said that "these signs will accompany those who believe: In my name they will drive out demons" (Mark 16:17 NIV).

You and I have His mandate to enforce the victory of the cross of Christ Jesus today.

Principles of Battle

There are three principles of battle we must stand upon as we step out in faith to destroy the works of the devil, our defeated foe: what happened *because* of the cross, *by* the cross, and *at* the cross.

Watch this now. This is critical!

Because of the cross, every person can receive forgiveness of sins, be in right standing with the Father, and enter into fellowship in favor with God. For those who accept this substitutionary work of Jesus, Satan has been deprived of his great weapon against God and man: sin, which results in separation between God and man.

But on the cross "the Lord laid on him the sins of us all" (Isaiah 53:6 NLT). God now forgives those who repent and put their faith in Christ and punishes Satan and his fallen angels for their usurping act of rebellion.

By the cross Christ accomplished three things: He defeated Satan, He took away Satan's legal authority to rule over man, and He restored the blessings Satan stole from mankind.

At the cross Jesus restored all that Satan had stolen. Satan is a thief, a deceiver, and the father of lies. He has never—and will never—play fair by the rules unless we, the Body of Christ, enforce the victory of Calvary.

Two consequences now follow:

- Satan will unceasingly strive to keep humans, and especially the Church, in a state of ignorance, darkness, weakness, disability, and division.
- We can overcome Satan and his descending ranks of darkness as we believe, proclaim, act out, and live out the triumph of Christ.

Our job is to expose the enemy's darkness by turning on the light of the completed work of the cross of Christ and enforcing the victory Jesus Christ historically has already won.

Using the words of Paul the apostle, let us give thanks to God, "who gives us the victory through our Lord Jesus Christ" and "always leads us in triumph in Christ, and through us reveals the fragrance of the knowledge of Him in every place" (1 Corinthians 15:57; 2 Corinthians 2:14). This is the inheritance for all who follow Jesus.

This brings an old hymn to my mind. "At the cross, at the cross, where I first saw the light, and the burden of my heart roll'd away, it was there by faith I receiv'd my sight, and now I am happy night and day."[1] Amen and amen!

FOR REFLECTION AND PRAYER

- What freedom have you experienced lately as a direct result of Jesus' sacrifice on the cross?
- What is one way you can turn on the light of the completed work of the cross?

Take a few moments right now to give thanks to Jesus for the work of the cross and all He has provided because of the cross, by the cross, and at the cross.

30

Barriers to Kingdom Advancement

As we move forward to enforce Christ's victory on the cross, we will encounter barriers that will hinder the advancement of the Kingdom of God. There are four key barriers I believe the Holy Spirit desires to help us overcome: relational issues with God, the devil, the Body of Christ, and with our theology. Let's look at each.

1. Relational issues with God

Despite years of church attendance and regular Bible reading, some believers still walk in ignorance of three key aspects of the Godhead: the love of the Father, the triumph of the Son, and the power of the Spirit.

Father God loves you and is for you (see John 3:16–17; Romans 8:31–29; James 1:17). Jesus rescued you, forgave you, and transferred you into His Kingdom (see Colossians 1:13–14). And the Holy Spirit desires to demonstrate the victory of Christ through you (see Acts 1:8; Ephesians 1:17–20). What I have just said is enough to explore and meditate on for a lifetime.

Not knowing God, His true nature and attributes, hinders us from advancing His Kingdom. This is why the apostle Paul encouraged the Church to always be "increasing in the knowledge of God" (Colossians 1:10). Don't let ignorance get in the way of you doing your part in the Kingdom. For "this is eternal life, that they may *know You*, the only true God, and Jesus Christ whom You have sent" (John 17:3, emphasis added).

2. Relational issues with the devil

We are not to be ignorant of the devil's schemes. This word *schemes* brings to mind an architect with blueprints, or schemata. When he was growing up, Dr. Bill Bright, founder of Campus Crusade of Christ, had little tracts that he composed. The most famous of all started off with a key statement: "God has a wonderful plan for your life!" Well, not only does God have a blueprint for your life, but the devil has a scheme laid out for you as well, and we are warned to not be ignorant concerning it.

We need to be aware of the wily tactics and relational temptations the deceiver cyclically uses. I see three issues in this regard that can become barriers to Kingdom advancement: we deny the work of the devil, we have common ground with the devil, and we fear the devil more than we should.

First, a western, liberal, modernistic world view denies the spiritual reality that there is a devil who "prowls around like a roaring lion, seeking someone to devour" (1 Peter 5:8). We Christians try to fit in and fear confronting the spirits behind the evil in our world and call it for what it is.

Second, we have "common ground" with the enemy that must be destroyed. We dabble (and sometimes fully engage) in sins and expect to have victory over the enemy. Someone cannot cast out a demon of lust when he entertains pornography in his private life. Jesus walked in the authority and power that He did because He had nothing in common with the prince of this world (see John 14:30). We must break any relational ties we have with evil so we can advance the Kingdom of God right through the gates of hell.

Lastly, when we engage in spiritual warfare, we may be tempted to pull away out of fear of backlash from the devil. Who wants to get wounded in the war? No one! But we can attribute more ability to the devil to attack us and deceive us than God's ability to protect us. Yes, we must walk wisely in battle, but we can walk courageously in the power of the Holy Spirit to advance the Kingdom of God.

3. Relational issues within the Body of Christ

There are also relational issues within the Body of Christ that create barriers to Kingdom advancement. I will highlight three: disvaluing unity, prayer, and church history.

First, seasoned spiritual leaders, often referred to as elders, are not sitting at the gate of their cities together in unity. Instead, they are competing against one another, mirroring the powers of darkness, which disvalues unity. Thankfully we have seen many congregations, ministries, churches, and marketplace leaders coming together on behalf of their cities, but we still have much room for growth.

Second, watchmen and gatekeepers are also often not walking in unity together, resulting in an atmosphere of displacement, which disvalues the authentic role of leaders of houses of prayer and worship. But we must humble ourselves and come to a place where we walk in a culture of honor and their success is our success.

Third, the Body of Christ is allowing sins of bitterness and historic injustices to persist. In past years the Church has gained ground in this area through identificational repentance (see my books *Intercession: The Power and Passion to Shape History* and *Strike the Mark* for more on this). With each new generation comes the opportunity for fresh offense and bitterness, which gives a legal basis for the demonic host to rule. Let's value Church history and learn from the past so we don't repeat the same unhealthy patterns that undermine the Church's strength.

4. Theological deficiencies that promote weakness

Three theological deficiencies can be a serious barrier to Kingdom advancement: cessationism, escapism, and an imbalance in belief about the sovereignty of God.

First, I believe cessationism is the devil's deception and a highly effective weapon in his arsenal. Cessationism is a false doctrine stating the gifts of the Holy Spirit stopped working with the closing of the canon of Scripture. This belief produces a Christianity with no power. The Holy Spirit whispered the following to me years ago when I was young in my pastoral ministry: "Your end time worldview will determine your lifestyle." I wondered what in the world that meant. I wish now that when I was that age, I'd understood it. That statement means a lot to me today. Enforcing the victory of Calvary requires the gifts and power of the Holy Spirit. Do not let this errant view be a barrier to Kingdom advancement in your life.

Second, escapism theories distort the Church's ultimate mission. The goal of Christians is not to get out of here when the going gets tough. Our goal is to get as much of God in here as we can while we are here. Jesus didn't teach His disciples to pray, "Lord, get us out," but rather Jesus taught His disciples to pray, "Thy kingdom come, Thy will be done in earth, as it is in heaven" (Matthew 6:10 KJV). The word the Holy Spirit spoke to me harkens us, "Your end time worldview will determine your lifestyle." We are to rule in the midst of our enemies, releasing Kingdom authority.

Third, there has been an imbalance concerning what we believe about the sovereignty of God. Yes, we have been "predestined according to the purpose of Him who works all things in accordance with the plan of His will" (Ephesians 1:11). But we have also been called to be "co-workers in God's service" and "co-heirs with Christ" to enforce the victory of Calvary (1 Corinthians 3:9;

Romans 8:17 NIV). How do we do that? We use our powerful spiritual weapons, which we have looked at extensively and will expand upon in the next chapter.

These four issues about God, the devil, the Body of Christ, and our theological deficiencies can only be barriers if we allow them to hinder us from advancing the Kingdom of God. Let's see them instead as hurdles to jump over as we run the race set out before us by our victorious King Jesus!

FOR REFLECTION AND PRAYER

- Which of these do you need a greater revelation of in order to fight more effectively as you advance God's Kingdom: the love of the Father, the triumph of the Son, or the power of the Spirit?

- When have you pulled away from a spiritual battle because you have feared backlash from the enemy?

- What is your role in the Body of Christ to help us value unity, prayer, and church history—and not repeat the same unhealthy patterns that undermine the Church's strength?

- How have the theological issues discussed above caused division between believers and kept us powerless?

Take a few moments right now to talk to God about barriers you see that get in the way of Kingdom advancement in your life. Then ask the Holy Spirit to empower you afresh for His glory and service.

31

ENFORCING THE VICTORY WITH WISDOM AND WEAPONS

In previous chapters I detailed various spiritual weapons God has given us to use to enforce the triumph of Christ. We've looked at the armor of God, the high praises of God, angels sent from God to help us, and the power of the blood at the cross of Christ and through receiving the Lord's Supper.

There are twelve more weapons I want to share with you. Some may be different than what you expect, but hopefully you will see that whatever the Holy Spirit gives us can be a divine weapon against the powers of darkness. Let me give you an example.

During a recent time of recovery from surgery, I had several people come and help. I've also had some work being done in my home. My posture toward these visitors has been to demonstrate love and kindness however I can. Are love and kindness spiritual weapons? Yes, they are! The fruit of the Spirit displaces works of darkness such as hate and fear.

When the heating and air conditioning man came, instead of getting him in and out as quickly as possible, I learned that he was very broken because his family has been caught in immigration difficulties. I did what I could to help him and give him hope. Another worker in my home noticed all my books and asked, "Would you maybe have some kind of Bible that doesn't have all the thees and thous in it?" It was my great joy to give him the Word of God in a modern translation.

We can all do things like this. Did I cast out a demon or battle a territorial spirit? No, but you know what? I exemplified the character of Christ and presented Him to those who do not yet know Him. The apostle Paul wrote, "But thanks be to God, who always leads us in triumph in Christ, and through us reveals the fragrance of the knowledge of Him in every place" (2 Corinthians 2:14). We triumph in Christ when we release the fragrance of Christ wherever we go. That is effective spiritual warfare.

More Powerful Weapons

Here are more powerful spiritual weapons God gives us to enforce Christ's victory. Which weapons surprise you? And which one can you see yourself using in the future?

1. The power of preaching (1 Corinthians 1:21; 2:4)
2. The gifts of the Spirit—word of wisdom, word of knowledge, faith, healing, power to perform miracles, prophecy, discerning of spirits, tongues, interpretation of tongues (1 Corinthians 12:8–10)
3. Shouts of grace (Zechariah 4:6–7)
4. God's presence (Joshua 5:13–15)
5. Unity (Psalm 133)
6. The power of confession of historic sins (Nehemiah 1:6–7; John 20:23)

7. Forgiveness and repentance (2 Chronicles 7:14; Matthew 6:12–15)
8. Acting in the opposite spirit (Micah 6:8)
9. Sacrifice (Psalm 50:23)
10. Watching and waiting (Isaiah 40:31; Matthew 26:41)
11. Authority from God (2 Kings 18:3–5; 23:4–5)
12. Loving the things God loves and honoring the things God honors (Genesis 12:3; Matthew 5:3–12; Luke 14:13–14)

Healing Wounds through Process Praying

What is process praying? Process praying is a form of praying that is not a one-time prayer that fixes everything. It is a united, intercessory effort that involves a good deal of process. We need to study and honor the efforts of those who have worked in these concerted areas previously. Process praying is a process that includes the efforts of those who have gone before us, those who are laboring in different streams, and noting that others might be a part of the process in the future.

Process praying also includes dialogue with one another and receiving insight from the Holy Spirit right on the spot—receiving, interpreting, and then bringing application to the now revelation of the Holy Spirit in our prayer process. Healing historic wounds especially requires process praying.

Over the years I have been involved in gatherings to deal systematically with strongholds, generational sins, and other issues that need to be resolved through corporate spiritual warfare. It is generally apparent what historic sins and traumas people and regions have endured and/or are still suffering from currently.

I had the honor of being a point person for one such gathering concerning the historic sins against the Cherokee, First Nations, and the injustices that remain for these people groups.

Representatives from all parties were there: descendants of the tribes and the settlers. I have also been engaged in multiple prayer journeys praying with insight on site for other targeted issues of injustices in various lands and nations. But I have typically been invited by leaders in those cities and nations and not just gone on my own. There is no room for solo acts in these realms!

These gatherings are typically more personal, and the tone can be a bit more somber and targeted. While this type of healing of wounds takes place layer by layer, authentic spiritual warfare ultimately deals with the root issues, dismantles strongholds, and brings cleansing and freedom to the people of the land and to the land itself.

The following is one possible model that may be applicable when you consider stepping out to enforce Calvary's victory in a situation like this:

1. Create a "war council" with those who are seasoned and personally invested, with leaders such as pastors, apostles, discerning watchmen, and other fivefold ministers who are willing to devote their time to walk relationally together and understand the goals of a meeting. This meeting takes time because all those involved must have a voice that can be heard. The culture of humility and honor is imperative.

2. Appoint a leader who understands the ultimate purpose of this gathering: repentance, forgiveness, healing, and reconciliation. This person may be a strategic-level intercessor or someone who understands the reality of dealing with territorial spirits.

3. Allow the Holy Spirit to highlight a facilitator who has special discernment. This may be the leader I mentioned above, or it could be a different person equipped with the grace to ensure the assembly understands all that is going on. This leader may or may not be part of the ambassadorial prayers or acts of repenting.

4. Host a solemn assembly prayer gathering. These are often private gatherings with an agreed upon guided process for repentance and forgiveness.

5. Repent and forgive. All sin is transgression against God, so ask Him first for forgiveness. Then there must be repentance to the descendants of those sinned against for acts against their ancestors, and acts against them, if applicable. Local leaders, acting as gatekeepers for that location, should represent those who sinned and those who were sinned against. All members need to participate wholeheartedly. Usually there are sins such as prejudice on both sides. Allow room for the Holy Spirit to move and for the process to evolve to completion.

The process might be slow, it might go deep, and it might take time. It is important to repent for destructive schisms, divisions, and competitions that are causing disunity. This is relational process praying at its core. Don't force the process—you are participating in the healing of generations. There is no way for me to describe the tears, the travail, the joy, and the release that comes from remitting sins. The process drains the anger of the oppressed through forgiveness and releases the shame from those who did the oppressing—which opened the gate of hell, in a sense, in a territory.

Complete healing probably will not happen in this one appointed gathering. You might even hit a ceiling. But always believe that every prayer counts and every sacrifice matters. Just don't quit!

Wisdom in Warfare

The process of forgiveness is connected to the process of spiritual warfare. Paul the apostle wrote, "Anyone you forgive, I also forgive. And what I have forgiven—if there was anything to forgive—I have forgiven in the sight of Christ for your sake, in order that Satan might not outwit us. For we are not unaware of his schemes" (2 Corinthians

2:10–11 NIV). One of Satan's schemes is to keep us bound by unforgiveness. He also has other schemes God calls us to discern, including accusation, distraction, intimidation, deception, despair, heresies, division, manipulation and control, confusion, and the like.

How can we take action? For all spiritual warfare I recommend the following five principles that will lead you wisely to enforce Christ's victory:

1. Become aware of his schemes (2 Corinthians 2:11; 2 Kings 6:8–23).

2. Become confident of your authority (Luke 10:19; 1 John 4:4; 1 Corinthians10:13).

3. Be prepared to defend yourself using the full armor of God (Ephesians 6:10–11).

4. Step out on the offensive, not just defensive (Matthew 11:12, 16; 18:20; Luke 14:14–22).

5. Speak more to God than to the enemy. Do not let the enemy be your focus; God is (Matthew 14:22–36).

I've stated this many times and I'll say it again: you were born in war, and you were born for war. If you feel you've lost to the enemy more than you've won, it's time for that to change. Jesus has already triumphed, and He has seated us with Him in the heavenly places.

He has positioned us by His side to have a perspective that enables us to enforce the victory of Calvary with wisdom utilizing His delegated powerful weapons for spiritual warfare. Amen and amen!

FOR REFLECTION AND PRAYER

- Which of the weapons in this chapter surprised you the most, and which do you want to put to good use immediately?

- How is the fruit of the Spirit a spiritual weapon for warfare?
- In your own spiritual warfare, who do you find yourself speaking to most often? God or the enemy? What changes do you want to make going forward?

Take a few moments right now to ask God for wisdom as you confront the enemy in spiritual warfare.

32

THE FINAL OUTCOME

When you're in the middle of a fight, sometimes it's hard to see why you're fighting. You just want to survive! In those moments you can look to Jesus, "who for the joy set before Him endured the cross" (Hebrews 12:2). Did you catch that? While Jesus was on the cross, He was thinking of the final outcome of His sacrifice.

Isaiah 59:15–19 (NLT) speaks prophetically of Jesus, the Messiah, His mission, and the summation of all things:

> Yes, truth is gone, and anyone who renounces evil is attacked. The LORD looked and was displeased to find there was no justice. He was amazed to see that no one intervened to help the oppressed. So he himself stepped in to save them with his strong arm, and his justice sustained him. He put on righteousness as his body armor and placed the helmet of salvation on his head. He clothed himself with a robe of vengeance and wrapped himself in a cloak of divine passion. He will repay his enemies for their evil deeds. His fury will fall on his foes. He will pay them back even to the ends of the earth. In the west, people will respect the name of the LORD; in the east, they will glorify him. For he will come like a raging flood tide driven by the breath of the LORD.

What a powerful passage of Scripture! This can be our pattern for how we engage in spiritual warfare: the Holy Spirit opens our eyes to see where there is no justice and calls us to step in; we put on our spiritual armor and release proclamations of faith to rebuke and command the enemy to stop his evil plans, pursuits, acts, and activities; we can do none of this in our own power and efforts so we cloth ourselves in the power of the Holy Spirit.

What is the result? Evil is defeated, and the fear of the Lord and His glory cover the earth! Amen and amen!

If you are in the middle of a battle right now, feeling weary and discouraged, or if you are standing with someone contending for breakthrough, I have a word for you: keep your hand to the plow, stay focused, and don't give up. Read the words of Paul in Ephesians 3:8–13:

> To me, the very least of all saints, this grace was given, to preach to the Gentiles the unfathomable riches of Christ, and to enlighten all people as to what the plan of the mystery is which for ages has been hidden in God, who created all things; so that the multifaceted wisdom of God might now be made known through the church to the rulers and the authorities in the heavenly places. This was in accordance with the eternal purpose which He carried out in Christ Jesus our Lord in whom we have boldness and confident access through faith in Him. Therefore I ask you not to become discouraged about my tribulations in your behalf, since they are your glory.

Paul admonishes "not to become discouraged" about what you may be witnessing another person go through. You may have been praying for this and working at that year after year in your country, state, region, and community. I, too, have pursued victory on some things for years and years. Sometimes I wonder why I keep trying. And then I see victory in an area! And I have a nudge from the Holy Spirit that confirms I was right to be faithful. You are too.

God has a plan and a purpose for your life, and it includes being mantled for victory in every spiritual battle.

The Final Triumph

As we approach the end of the age, we know demonic activity will continue to increase. The book of Revelation, which captures John's vision of the future, describes demonic activity he saw, and what I believe we can expect:

- Demons are worshiped in the guise of idols (Revelation 9:20).
- Pagan religions are manifestations of Satan (Revelation 2:13).
- False teachings are inspired by Satan (Revelation 2:24).
- The devil motivates the persecution and martyrdom of the Christians (Revelation 2:10).
- Satan is the ruler behind the scenes for the antichrist (Revelation 13:1–14; Revelation 19:19).
- Demons are released to torment men (Revelation 9:1–11).
- Demons are behind war (Revelation 16:13–14).
- Demons fill the religious and political system called Babylon (Revelation 18:2), a type of world system organized independent of God with Satan at its head.

For those without the hope of Christ, this is a gloomy forecast. "But the people who know their God shall be strong, and carry out great exploits" (Daniel 11:32 NKJV). This is *our* future! This is *your* future!

While I have touched on the words of the apostle John in Revelation 12:11 earlier in this book, I want to revisit the revelation that shows what caused Satan, the fallen angels, and the demons to be overcome: "They triumphed over him by the blood of the Lamb and by the word of their testimony; they did not love their lives so much as to shrink from death" (NIV). Our final triumph has three important parts, which this verse clearly states. Let's look at each to learn how we will overcome and triumph.

1. The blood of the Lamb

Jesus Christ shed His precious, perfect blood for our sins in His atoning death at Calvary. His blood speaks better things than the innocent blood of Abel (Hebrews 12:24). Jesus' blood cries for mercy for us, not judgment. It is by His blood that we have been redeemed from Satan (see Ephesians 1:7; Psalm 106:10).

By His blood our sins have been forgiven, thereby removing Satan's base of accusation (see Ephesians 1:7; Colossians 2:13–15). Jesus' blood has justified us (see Romans 5:9). His blood sanctifies and sets us apart unto God (see Hebrews 13:12). And by the blood of Jesus heaven has been opened, the very throne of the Father, for us to come and have intimate fellowship with Him (see Hebrews 9:22–24; 10:19–22).

2. The word of our testimony

God wants you to share your testimony, and doing so will help you overcome. What is your testimony? Jesus is your testimony— the One who has destroyed the works of the devil and has brought you out of darkness into His marvelous light!

Let's be clear that we are each called to declare, confess, or testify what the blood of Jesus has already accomplished for us on the cross. Remember? By the blood of Jesus I am forgiven, cleansed, sanctified, justified, redeemed out of darkness, have peace, and have access to the throne of God so the accuser of the brethren is cast down!

What has Jesus done in your life? Testify. How do you testify? You testify by being a witness to what you have seen God do in your life. Has He healed you? Testify. Has He saved you? Share the Good News with others. Has He delivered you? Find someone else who is bound and declare the mighty power of Jesus to that person so he or she can be free.

When you remind yourself of what God has done and share your testimony as a witness of God's faithfulness, the Holy Spirit empowers you to overcome even in the darkest days. I should warn you, however, that the word for *witness* in Greek is *martus*, from which we get the word *martyr*. Being a witness implies being one who testifies of Christ even if it costs death. Let's look at the third part of Revelation 12:11.

3. Not loving our lives, even unto death

Closely linked with the first two parts of Revelation 12:11, we find a most necessary prerequisite for being a spiritual soldier is the willingness to die. When Jesus spoke of the coming of the Holy Spirit, He said, "But you will receive power when the Holy Spirit comes upon you. And you will be my witnesses, telling people about me everywhere" (Acts 1:8 NLT).

The power to lead lives as martyr-witnesses enabled the early Church to quickly expand and dethrone the demonic strongholds (see Acts 8:1–8). Consider a few examples of martyrs who chose not to love their lives even unto death. John the Baptist was such a witness (see Mark 6:14–29). Stephen too, according to Acts 7:54–60. Revelation 2:13 speaks of Antipas, whom Jesus called, "My witness [martyr], My faithful one." The apostles were such witnesses (see John 21:18–23; 2 Timothy 4:6–8, 14–18).

The key to being a faithful witness, even unto death, is to follow the example of Paul who said, "I die daily" (1 Corinthians 15:31). According to Acts 20:24, Paul said, "I do not consider my life of any account as dear to myself, so that I may finish my course and the ministry which I received from the Lord Jesus, to testify solemnly of the gospel of God's grace." You can see the three elements of Revelation 12:11 in this verse: the sacrifice of Jesus, testifying of God's grace, and the sacrifice of self.

It is the blood of the saints and the blood of the martyrs of Jesus that precipitated the destruction of Babylon (see Revelation 17:6). From this we see that the blood of the Lamb that speaks in heaven also flows through His Body on the earth. When a martyr is slain, it is Jesus' blood that flows afresh. The judgments of God are loosed against the demons whenever they cause a saint to die. God's weapons are disciples fully yielded to the Holy Spirit, with no other agenda than to do the will of Jesus.

Finishing Well

I have a goal to finish well. My goal is to be a man of integrity and a person of prayer. My goal is to hear God and teach others how to hear God for themselves. My goal is to help raise up an army of God who in turn will know that their lives matter and that they are called to be enforcers in the Kingdom of God. That's you!

You are why I wrote this book because you are called to testify to what the Lord Jesus has done and enforce the victory He has won.

While our stories are in the making, they already have an ending secured by Christ for those who choose to follow Him and endure till the end. Satan has already been judged (see John 16:11). The Church, the loyal Bride, will become part of the triumphant army to return with the Lamb-Lion of God and defeat the enemy once and for all (see Revelation 19–21). His ending is the lake of fire, along with all his legions (see Revelation 20:10, 14–15; Matthew 25:40–41).

Then Jesus "will wipe away every tear from their eyes; and there will no longer be any death; there will no longer be any mourning, or crying, or pain" (Revelation 21:4). "There will no longer be any curse," says Revelation 22:3. Spiritual warfare as we know it today will cease and "so we will be with the Lord forever" (1 Thessalonians 4:17). But until that day, we work with the heavenly host to enforce Christ's victory with the many weapons He gives us.

What is the ultimate key to being effective in spiritual warfare? Why, it's looking unto Jesus, the author and perfector of our faith! "And this is the victory has overcome the world: our faith" (1 John 5:4).

Make this final declaration with me from Revelation 5:5: "The Lion of the tribe of Judah, the Root of David, has triumphed." And because of Jesus, we triumph with Him. Amen and amen!

FOR REFLECTION AND PRAYER

- What kind of demonic activity are you seeing on the earth today? How does Revelation 12:11 provide our response to this evil?
- The Holy Spirit gives you the power to live a martyr-witness life to dethrone demonic strongholds (Acts 8:1–8). What does that type of lifestyle look like to you?
- What does finishing well look like to you?

VICTORIOUS SPIRITUAL WARFARE PRAYER

Magnificent heavenly Father, I want Your fame and glory to be spread throughout all the earth. I agree that only one name should be lifted up above every other—the name of Jesus. I agree that every tongue should confess only one name—the name of Jesus. Jesus has changed everything.

Thank You, Jesus, that You took my sin upon Yourself so I could be made righteous. Thank You, Jesus, for becoming a curse so I could receive the abundance of my Father's blessings.

Because of the shed blood at Calvary, I am a recipient of Your great grace. Jesus, when You declared from the cross, "It is finished," Your work was complete. Now, as a New Testament believer, I am called to be an enforcer of Your victory. I take my place in Your army with the blood of the Lamb, the word of my testimony, and I lay my life down for You daily so that You can live through me. For this weighty task, I receive the grace of my Lord Jesus Christ, the love of God the Father, and the communion of the Holy Spirit, who is with me until the end. Amen and amen.

Notes

Chapter 1 The Great Battle Between Two Kingdoms

1. C. S. Lewis, *The Screwtape Letters* (New York; Macmillan, 1982), 3. *The Screwtape Letters* by CS Lewis © copyright 1942 CS Lewis Pte Ltd. Extract used with permission.

Chapter 4 Angels 101

1. Martin Luther, *The Table-Talk of Martin Luther*, trans. and ed. William Hazlitt, Esq. (London: Bell & Daldy, 1872), 245.

2. John Calvin, *Institutes of the Christian Religion Vol. I*, trans. John Allen (Philadelphia: Presbyterian Board of Christian Education, 1936), 183–184.

3. "Angels," Catholic Online, accessed September 2, 2022, https://www.catholic.org/saints/angels.

4. Geoffrey Dennis, *The Encyclopedia of Jewish Myth, Magic and Mysticism* (Woodbury: Llewellyn Publications, 2007), 13.

5. Billy Graham, *Angels: God's Secret Agents* (Garden City: Doubleday & Company, Inc., 1975), 18.

6. My book *Angelic Encounters* will expose you to a broader lens on this topic. But according to non-Apocrypha materials, the canon of Scripture, we only find Lucifer, Gabriel, and Michael.

Chapter 6 The Snare of Pride and Insecurity

1. Even more in-depth discussions can be found in my books *Deliverance from Darkness* and *The Discerner*.

Chapter 9 The Hierarchy of Satan's Dominion

1. I encourage you to read my book and curriculum kit materials on *The Discerner*, which delve more into this very enlightening subject.

2. Ed Silvoso, *That None Should Perish: How to Reach Entire Cities for Christ Through Prayer Evangelism* (Ventura: Regal Books, 1995), 154.

3. I refer you to *Strike the Mark* and *Prayers that Strike the Mark*, the book and set of materials where I methodically go through the legal basis of the rights of the powers of the air to rule.

4. Silvoso, *That None Should Perish*, 154.

Section 5 Christ's Triumph—the Devil's Defeat

1. Stephen S. Smalley, *1, 2, 3 John*, Word Biblical Commentary 51 (Waco: Word, 1984), 170.

Chapter 10 How Jesus Destroyed the Devil's Works

1. See my book *Deliverance from Darkness* that delves into this subject extensively.

2. John Piper, *The Pleasures of God: Meditations on God's Delight in Being God* (Colorado Springs: Multnomah Books, 2000), 165.

Section 6 Your Warfare Weapons

1. "He Lives" is one of the most favorite Easter hymns, written by Alfred H. Ackley (1887–1960) on Easter night in 1932. "He Lives," Rev. A. H. Ackley, *Triumphant Service Songs* (Chicago: Rodeheaver-Hall Mack, 1934), 286.

Chapter 13 How We Can Be Strong

1. Clinton E. Arnold, *Powers of Darkness: Principalities and Powers in Paul's Letters* (Downers Grove: InterVarsity Press, 1992), 27–28.

2. Clinton E. Arnold, *Power and Magic: The Concept of Power in Ephesians* (Grand Rapids: Baker Books, 1997), 117.

Chapter 15 The Power Behind the Armor

1. Silvoso, *That None Should Perish*, 154.

2. I suggest reading my book *The Lost Art of Practicing His Presence* and the corresponding curriculum kit, where I discuss the transmitter and receiver and how to turn it off and on.

3. William Cowper, "What Various Hindrances We Meet," 1779, public domain.

Chapter 16 Truth and Righteousness

1. George Mallone, *Arming for Spiritual Warfare: How Christians Need to Recognize and Fight the Enemy within the Church* (Eagle Guildford, Surrey: Eagle, 1991), 28.

2. Ibid, 29.

3. Derek Prince, "The Breastplate of Righteousness," transcript, Derek Prince Ministries, accessed September 18, 2023, https://www.derekprince.com/radio/677.

4. Ibid.

Chapter 18 Inspiration from Joshua and Jonah

1. You may want to read more about this topic in my book *Global Prayer Storm*.

Chapter 24 The Significance of the Lord's Supper

1. Jonathan Black, *The Lord's Supper: Our Promised Place of Intimacy and Transformation with Jesus* (Minneapolis: Chosen Books, 2023), 30–31.
2. Lewis E. Jones, *Power in the Blood*, 1899, public domain.

Chapter 25 How We Overcome by the Blood

1. Derek Prince, "By This I Overcome the Devil," Derek Prince Ministries, accessed September 19, 2023, https://www.derekprince.com/cards/c-pc03-100.
2. Charles Spurgeon, "Pleading," The Spurgeon Center for Biblical Preaching at Midwestern Seminary, October 28, 1871, https://www.spurgeon.org/resource-library/sermons/pleading/#flipbook/.

Chapter 26 The Territoriality of the Demonic Host

1. You can read more about encounters like this in my book *Angelic Encounters* and corresponding material.

Chapter 27 Spiritual Mapping

1. George Otis, Jr., *The Last of the Giants: Lifting the Veil on Islam and the End Times* (Tarrytown: Chosen Books, 1991), 85.
2. Harold Caballeros, "Defeating the Enemy with the Help of Spiritual Mapping," *Breaking Spiritual Strongholds in Your City*, ed. C. Peter Wagner, (Tunbridge Wells: Monarch, 1993), 125.
3. C. Peter Wagner, "Summary: Mapping Your Community," *Breaking Spiritual Strongholds in Your City*, ed. C. Peter Wagner, (Tunbridge Wells: Monarch, 1993), 224.
4. Cindy Jacobs, "Dealing with Strongholds," *Breaking Spiritual Strongholds in Your City*, ed. C. Peter Wagner, (Tunbridge Wells: Monarch, 1993), 80–81.
5. Kjell Sjöberg, "Spiritual Mapping for Prophetic Prayer Actions," *Breaking Spiritual Strongholds in Your City*, ed. C. Peter Wagner, (Tunbridge Wells: Monarch, 1993), 99.
6. Kjell Sjöberg, *Winning the Prayer War* (Chinchester: Sovereign World, 1991), 60.

Chapter 28 How to Wisely Confront Powers of Darkness

1. C. Peter Wagner, *Spiritual Warfare Strategy: Confronting Spiritual Powers* (Shippensburg: Destiny Image Publishers, 2011), 98.

Chapter 29 The Work of the Cross and Principles of Battle

1. R. Kelso Carter, "At the Cross," 1896, public domain.

ABOUT THE AUTHOR

James W. Goll is the founder of God Encounters Ministries and Global Prayer Storm. He is an international bestselling author, an adviser to leaders and ministries, and a recording artist. James has traveled around the world ministering in more than fifty nations sharing the love of Jesus—imparting the power of intercession, prophetic ministry, and life in the Spirit. He has recorded numerous classes with corresponding curriculum kits and is the author of more than fifty books, including *The Lifestyle of a Prophet*, *The Lost Art of Intercession*, *The Seer*, *The Discerner*, and *The Mystery of Israel and the Middle East*.

James was married to Michal Ann for thirty-two years before her graduation to heaven in the fall of 2008. He has four adult married children and a growing number of grandchildren. His goal is to "win for the Lamb the rewards of His suffering." James makes his home in Franklin, Tennessee.

For More Information

James W. Goll
God Encounters Ministries
P.O. Box 681965
Franklin, TN 37068
Phone: 1-877-200-1604
Office: 615-599-5552

Websites:
GodEncounters.com
GlobalPrayerStorm.com
MentoringWithJames.com/GEM

Email Address:
info@GodEncounters.com
linktr.ee/GodEncounters

Social Media Sites:
Facebook.com: @JamesGollPage and
@GodEncountersMinistries
Instagram: @JamesGoll and @GodEncounters
YouTube: @JamesGollOfficial
Apple Podcasts: *God Encounters Today Podcast*
Rumble.com/c/SeekingInsight
Vimeo.com/JamesGoll
GEM Media
XPMedia.com/channel/encounter293
KingdomFlame.com/tag/james-goll